DOWNRIVER

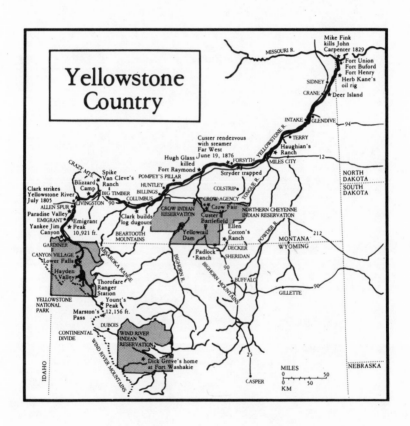

·DOWNRIVER·
A Yellowstone Journey

DEAN KRAKEL II

SIERRA CLUB BOOKS   SAN FRANCISCO

The Sierra Club, founded in 1892 by John Muir, has devoted itself to the study and protection of the earth's scenic
and ecological resources—mountains, wetlands, wood-
lands, wild shores and rivers, deserts and plains. The pub-
lishing program of the Sierra Club offers books to the public as a nonprofit educational service in the hope that they
may enlarge the public's understanding of the Club's basic
concerns. The point of view expressed in each book, however, does not necessarily represent that of the Club. The
Sierra Club has some sixty chapters coast to coast, in Canada, Hawaii, and Alaska. For information about how you
may participate in its programs to preserve wilderness and
the quality of life, please address inquiries to Sierra Club,
730 Polk Street, San Francisco, CA 94109.

Copyright © 1987 by Dean Krakel II
Sierra Club Books paperback edition: 1988

LIBRARY OF CONGRESS CATALOGING-IN-PUBLICATION DATA

Krakel, Dean, 1952–
Downriver : a Yellowstone journey.

1. Yellowstone National Park.   2. Yellowstone River—
Description and travel.   3. Yellowstone River Valley—
History.   4. Krakel, Dean, 1952–   —Journeys—
Yellowstone River.   I. Title.
F722.K72   1987   917.87'520433   86–22087
ISBN 0–87156–785–7

COVER DESIGN BY WILSTED & TAYLOR
BOOK DESIGN BY WILSTED & TAYLOR
YELLOWSTONE MAP BY DIANE ESSINGTON
PRINTED IN THE UNITED STATES OF AMERICA
10 9 8 7 6 5 4 3 2 1

This book is for my son,
DEAN,
in hopes that there will be wild rivers
and wild country for him to roam.

"If there is still magic left upon this planet, then it is contained in moving water." LOREN EISELEY

"A whole river that is really a river is much to comprehend unless it is the Mississippi or the Danube or the Yangtze-Kiang and you spend a lifetime in its navigation; and even then what you comprehend, probably, are channels and topography and perhaps the honkytonks in the river's towns. A whole river is mountain country and hill country and flat country and swamp and delta country, is rock bottom and sand bottom and weed bottom and mud bottom, is blue, green, red, clear, brown, wide, narrow, fast, slow, clean and filthy water, is all the kinds of trees and grasses and all the breeds of animals and birds and men that pertain and have ever pertained to its changing shores, is a thousand differing and not compatible things in-between that point where enough of the highlands drainlets have trickled together to form it, and that wide, flat, probably desolate place where it discharges itself into the salt of the sea . . ." JOHN GRAVES

Contents

Acknowledgments

Numerous people contributed to my knowledge of the Yellowstone over the years and I am grateful to them all. Knowing that book acknowledgments all too often become impersonal lists I have tried to express my appreciation to those individuals in person rather than mentioning them here. Some of the people who helped in my understanding of the river became a part of the story and are mentioned in the text, so I'll not repeat their names again.

Few people know the Yellowstone better or love it more than Bob Wiltshire who runs the Crazy Mountain Raft Company out of Emigrant, Montana. The many river days and camps and conversations we shared will always be among my most cherished memories. The same can be said of my friends Tom Brown, John Stillman, and John Fryer, faithful partners in all kinds of endeavors. Livingston fishing guide Ray Hurley not only gave freely of his time and knowledge but tried in vain to make a fly fisherman of me. Officials of Yellowstone Park were always helpful, especially rangers Tim Blank and Rodger Rudolph. Rancher Walley McCrae of Colstrip, Montana gave me valuable insights into the effects of strip mining on ranching as did staff members of the Northern Plains Resource Council in Billings. Sam Scott of Decker Mines, Decker, Montana and Wes Bedker of Western Energy Mines, Colstrip, Montana answered numerous questions. Dan Scott Sr. and Dan Scott Jr. of Dayton, Wyoming, owners of the Padlock Ranch, gave me free rein in their domain. Oldtown Canoe and Phoenix Kayak companies both donated boats to the cause; I used both the canoe and kayak in early trips but in the end found that a raft was more suited to my needs. The Montana Fish and Game Department gave aid whenever it was needed. I might not have had a river to write about if not for their efforts to keep it free. Special thanks to Bill Pryor. The late Conrad Schweiring and his wonderful wife Mary Ethel of Jackson, Wyoming always gave me support when it was most needed. Connie's presence in my life is greatly missed. Angus Cameron gave me early encouragement with the manuscript as did Bobbie Bristol. Without their kind words I might have abandoned it several times. I count myself extremely fortunate to have had Angus as a mentor and friend. Ellen Levine had faith that the manuscript would be published. My editor, Jim Cohee, let it be.

My wife Alisa and son Dean are so much a part of this work that I find it impossible to express the thanks I feel in my heart for their many sacrifices and contributions. Jennie, my sister, and my brother Jack never let me forget what was most important along the path. Jennie's husband, Stan, contributed much towards my Yellowstone education. My father, Dean Sr., urged me to begin this book and helped see it through. The support of him and my mother, Iris, saw us through many storms. Donna Meade, my mother-in-law, provided an inspiring example of personal strength.

Many of my Yellowstone experiences were made possible by National Geographic Magazine. Special thanks to former Director of Photography Robert Gilka and Illustrations Editor Bob Patton.

Introduction

In 1976 I moved to Livingston, Montana to begin work on a book about the Yellowstone River. The river was in some danger of being dammed or otherwise ruined then—it is the last major free-flowing river left in America—and I wanted to see it and tell its story before it was too late.

When I first came to the river I thought of it in terms of landscape, as a thread with which to weave chapters together. I had never been in a boat, or really given much thought to water. Because the Yellowstone is paralleled by a highway for much of its seven hundred mile length I assumed that most of my research would be conducted from the bank.

But there came a time when the current's pull proved irresistible, no bridge or scenic turnout close enough, the river a mystery always bending from view. Its voice created an ache inside of me that only the going could satisfy. This is the story of such a going, a journey down the Yellowstone from its source on Yount's Peak in Wyoming's Absaroka Mountains to its confluence with the

Missouri River near the site of old Fort Union in North Dakota.

Although this is a work of nonfiction, it contains some fictionalizing. I have not tampered with fact. And I have tried to relate historical and contemporary occurrences truthfully. But during the course of my time along the Yellowstone I have had many experiences that I felt important to include in this book. In that vein I have taken liberties with certain characters, events, and circumstances to better suit my purpose.

I always supposed that when it came time to do this introduction I would be able to write some kind of crystalline distillation of what the Yellowstone is. But after nearly ten years of thinking and writing about it, of traveling upon and along it, the river remains an enigma. In the end, who's to say if what we perceive of a river, if what we comprehend, is something of its nature or our own.

Dean Krakel II
Pinedale, Wyoming 1986

Headwaters

AUGUST TWENTY-SIX

A TYPICAL START: IT'S NOON WHEN WE ARRIVE AT YEL-
lowstone Park. "Hope you're not planning to stay," says
the rangerette at the North Gate, "we're full." Taking
our place in a long line of traffic going south, we creep
bumper to bumper toward Old Faithful amidst the last
throes of summer tourist madness: drivers with glazed
eyes behind the windshields of vast Winnebagoes and
camper pickups making the Grand Tour, slamming on
the brakes to study any distant black speck that might
prove to be an animal. "Zat one a' them bizzon I been a'
hearin' bout?" a lady with pink framed sunglasses asks
me in passing, jerking her thumb in the direction of a
moose.

"Move along. Move along," says a tinny bullhorn
voice from the patrol car idling behind us.

At Lake Ranger Station we stop to obtain backcountry permits. "We close at five," says the ranger, "come
back tomorrow." But I insist—we're leaving tomorrow—until he reluctantly brings out the forms. Difficulties arise immediately.

"Point of origin?" asks Ranger, pen poised.

"Dubois, Wyoming," say I.

"That's not in the park."

"No sir."

"Well, suppose you tell me your itinerary. You're aware, of course, that campsites in Yellowstone are reserved only forty-eight hours in advance."

Itinerary? Isn't that one of the things we're trying to escape? Reservations? We have no idea of when we'll arrive anywhere, or how long we'll stay. What if there's a storm? What if we get lost or want to explore? The best I can do is to outline our general plan: we're horse-packing from Dubois to Yount's Peak. From there, my wife Alisa, son Dean, and I are going to follow the Yellowstone River, afoot, down to Yellowstone Lake. We'll have been riding a week and hiking a week before we cross Yellowstone Park's south boundary.

"The boy's only five," I say. "We're not sure how far he'll get each day."

Looking down over the counter at Dean, then at Alisa, then at me, Ranger's eyebrows arch beneath his Smokey Bear hat. Though he says nothing, the shadow of a doubt clouds his face. A decision requiring headquarters.

While the radio crackles with the chain of command, Alisa and I plot tentative dates and locations on the office map, a topographic covering a wall with several thousand square scale miles of green and brown contours. Numerous things to read on the walls as well: an orange TRAIL CLOSED/DANGEROUS BEAR sign with a fierce-looking grizzly drawn on it. Below that is a smaller WARNING/YELLOWSTONE IS BEAR COUNTRY sign.

"If you play dead," I read in a brochure titled *Hiking in Bear Country*, "the bear may give you only a few half-hearted slaps." ("Bear wants me, damned if I'll lay down and make it easy for him," an oldtimer once told me.) There are printed warnings about the hot water in geyser basins, the cold water in lakes, *Giardia* in the streams, and hypothermia in the climate. Beneath a Polaroid of a tent ripped apart by a hungry bear is handwritten "Don't let this happen to you."

Permission granted. We're read our rights in an official monotone: fire in the fire ring, no pets, no firearms, hang your food in a tree, boil the water, pack out your trash. Check in at the Thorofare patrol cabin.

"By the way," Ranger says as we turn toward the door, "there's been a Griz hitting camps at Bridger Lake."

Out the window to the east, across the lake's whitecaps, the Absaroka Mountains rear on the horizon like teeth.

It's dark by the time we reach Press Stephen's cabin outside Dubois. Supper's warmed in the wood stove. We eat outside on the porch by star light, to the sound of crickets and creeks and willows blowing, while Press traces our route across maps with his finger, speaking of drainages, passes, and mountain ranges all a mystery. He calls Yount's Peak, "world's center."

Press is twenty-eight, wears boots, Levi's, suspenders, and a checkered flannel shirt, smells of horses and leather and pine. He was born in Venezuela while his father was working for Coca-Cola. He still occasionally dreams in Spanish. The family moved to Georgia when he was eight. He attended Eastern boarding schools, graduated from Maine's Bowdoin College with an art history degree. But his fate was to fall in love with Wyoming's mountains during a summer vacation, and he went to work wrangling dudes and packing mules for the Triangle X Ranch in Jackson Hole, learning the trails from the Turner brothers, Harold, John, and Don, from the likes of Ike and Tommy Breen, Bill Daniels, and Jack Davis. Last year he started outfitting dudes on his own. "I'm a very small businessman," says Press.

We sort and pack late into the night, Press rattling pots and panniers in the barn loft, Alisa, Dean, and I stuffing duffel until we can stuff no more, then spreading our sleeping bags on the cabin floor.

By sunrise the loads have been sorted, weighed, balanced, hung, tarped, and hitched, and we're moving, packhorses blowing, jerking, and farting through the sagebrush. Press leads, riding Nephi; Ritz, Sugar, Sticker, and Cayuse roped nose to tail behind. Alisa follows on Kitty, the only mare. Dean bounces past at a trot on Dan, hands clenching saddle horn, speechless with terror and wonder—his first horseback ride. His guardian cowboy, William Little, gallops in hot pursuit. "The reins!" Bill's hollering. "Pull back on the reins!" But the reins, alas, drag the ground. Next comes wrangler Jack Swenson, on Nixon, leading Maynard (named for his beat goatee), Ziggy, Lawyer (the horse with no brains), Frog, and Hopeless (who truly is). Stout mountain horses, long of leg, deep of chest, slightly swaybacked, and sure of hoof. So we hope. "Uglier the packhorse the better," Press says.

Within a few miles we cross the east fork of Dunoir Creek. The Dunoir, Press tells me, is the Wind River's largest tributary. The Wind River becomes the Bighorn. Water muddied by our horses' hooves would have once reached the Yellowstone. Now, Boysen Reservoir plugs the Wind River; Yellowtail Dam the Bighorn.

At noon we begin switchbacking up through a dense lodgepole forest. The day grows cloudy, colder, the Absaroka changing from distant forms to a confusing jumble of deadfall, boulder, and slope.

We camp just shy of Shoshone Pass's nine-thousand-foot crest in a cool timberline drizzle. Standing around the supper fire, they in yellow slickers, we in ponchos, talk the small talk of strangers getting acquainted.

William Little, who'll lead our saddle horses back, is a jovial man in his early thirties with a blonde mustache; a part-time professor, free-lance cowboy, and aspiring painter. Reference is made to his Woodstock days. And for a time he ran a paramedical service on the Wind River Indian Reservation.

Jack Swenson has a degree in wildlife biology; a practicing ornithologist with a hawk's bright eyes and sharp features in a lean, unshaven face. He wintered in South America touring Mayan ruins and spent the spring counting nesting birds near the Bering Sea.

This evening's an anniversary of sorts for Press. Ten years ago he camped here on a packtrip with his first bunch of dudes.

"You want to find me in ten more years, just look right here."

We fall asleep to the music of horse bells, the intermittent tapping of rain on the tent fly.

As we're packing the horses this morning, three riders enter camp. A granddad, son, and grandson. So it appears. All are mounted on mules, looking for a mule they lost off Cougar Pass three days ago. "Mule must've rolled five hundred feet," the old man says. "Scattered the packs ta hell. Twisted the kid's new rifle into a pretzel. At the bottom, damn mule got up and run off." Information's exchanged (yup, nope, you bet) as a Skoal can makes the rounds. "Thanks," says Bill, taking a big pinch.

"I needed that. Forgot my own."

"Keep it," the kid says, "we're well supplied."

We climb from rain into mist. Shoshone Pass proves to be a narrow trail running at the edge of a gorge high above the silent white thread of Shoshone River's north fork. Gray clouds hang low over the mountains' heads; pine forests, a hundred shades of brightly wetted green, spread at their feet. Stones loosened by horses' hooves clatter into space. Twice I'm unnerved by the slick trail and dismount.

"Hold on tight," I tell Dean as he passes by. "Don't you sneeze, you old bastard," to Dan.

The pass is named for the Shoshone. Descendants of Aztecs, blood relatives to Comanches, Shoshone people

6

lived in basin lands scattered from here to California and south into Texas and Mexico, the most widely distributed and culturally diverse of all Native American linguistic families. We generally tend to think of Indians as mounted. But the people walked for the longest time.

It is told that when the Shoshone living on Wind River got the horse, sometime in the seventeenth century, they immediately raced north to make war on the Piegan. And though the Piegan were awed tremendously by those wondrous Big Dogs, they in turn introduced the Shoshone to bullets.

The mounted Shoshone may have occasionally passed through the Absaroka, but these mountains were home only to the Tukudiaka, poor relations who never acquired or never got on with the horse. Sheepeaters. There were never more than several hundred, living in huts of willow and bark, in holes and caves in these cliffs, as hardy as Bushmen, as shy as wolves.

When Yellowstone Park was created in 1872, there being no provision for wild people, as there was for scenery, the Sheep-eaters were removed to the Wind River Reservation and placed under the care of the great Shoshone Chief, Washakie.

The Shoshone named the river Stinking Water for the sulphuric taint given it by a geyser basin near present day Cody. Some historians claim that John Colter's hell was on the Shoshone, not in Yellowstone.

John Colter came into the Yellowstone country with Meriwether Lewis and William Clark as a private, age

7

twenty-four, fitting to perfection their modest enlist-
ment requirements for "good hunters, stout, healthy,
unmarried men, accustomed to the woods and capable
of bearing bodily fatigue in a pretty considerable degree."

On the expedition's return they met a canoe coming
upriver—Forest Hancock and Joseph Dixon, two Illi-
nois hunters heading west to trap beaver. They'd been
out a year already. Dixon had an Arikara arrow wound
in his leg. Lewis blessed them with some bacon and
lead, instructions as to where they might find beaver,
and bid them good luck. When the hunters paddled off,
John Colter went along.

It's thought he wintered with his partners somewhere on the Clark's fork; all that's known is that the
next spring he came paddling solo down the Missouri
bumping into Manuel Lisa's keelboat (some say two) at
the mouth of the Platte.

Lisa was first to act upon the news Lewis and Clark
brought. He planned to build a trading post on the Missouri. Colter turned him up the Yellowstone to the Bighorn's mouth where, that October, Fort Raymond was
constructed—two log huts and a palisade, the first
buildings in the Yellowstone Basin. And just in case the
Indios weren't already aware, Lisa dispatched Colter to
generate business.

Carrying a thirty pound pack and his rifle, Colter set
off alone on a winter odyssey that's been the marrow of
countless campfire speculation ever since. It's said he
was the first white man to see Wind River Valley, the

Teton Mountains, Yellowstone Lake, and the geysers of Yellowstone Park. He may have crossed the Absaroka by way of Shoshone Pass. But no one really knows. Colter kept no journal, authored no books, and if he bragged, no one recalled. He died of jaundice on a Missouri farm at the age of thirty-five.

The Shoshone River's stinking springs now lie at the bottom of Buffalo Bill Reservoir.

Clouds break into blue sky at the pass's bottom. We lunch in Bliss Creek Meadows in the shade of a boulder, watching brook trout hold in clear riffles of the Shoshone.

"It wasn't called Bliss out of happiness, you know," says Press, spreading peanut butter on bread with a Buck knife, "but for the horse thief Jack Bliss, hung from a pine here by a posse of outraged Cody citizens in 1892." Jack Bliss's packhorse wintered with a band of elk.

Riding away, we pass a white sign posted in a meadow, the number 81 and an arrow pointing east in red stencil. "Oil rig," Press says nonchalantly. "A young guy on an earlier trip said he had an oil lease around here somewhere. Everyone thought he was kidding— you can't drill for oil in a national forest. But he brought out a map and sure enough, he did."

"It'll be something new to look at," says Bill cynically, "it's so boring, same old trees and mountains all the time."

Leaving the Shoshone, we begin climbing toward Marston Pass. Aptly named Wall Mountain rises to our

left. Every hundred yards we pause precariously between switchbacks to rest the horses. I can look straight
up at Press's boot soles, straight down onto Jack's hat.

Afternoon becomes evening and pine shadows grow
cold. The Wall turns red with alpenglow. Dean nods in
the saddle; I squawk along behind keeping him awake.
We camp in a meadow crannied among boulders, so
high it takes all of Marston Creek to fill a water bucket.

A rest day. But for the horses, not us. Bellies full of pancakes, we're off to scale a ridge and reconnoiter Marston
Pass through binoculars. The trail often washes out and
Forest Service crews seldom make it back this far. Press
wants no surprises tomorrow.

Hopping boulder to boulder up the creekbed we
gain the snowfields and talus slopes above timberline.
Press wears $3 tennis shoes, carries Dean on his shoul-
ders. The man must possess the lungs and legs of a bighorn sheep. I'm soon left behind.

While I'm eating a sandwich, sitting on the snow at
the edge of a steep slope, an ermine carrying a dead
mouse almost runs over my outstretched legs. Startled,
we both drop our lunches and freeze. Our staring
match ends when I'm distracted by an ominous peal of
thunder. When I look back the ermine's gone.

The rain begins so suddenly I'm soaked before I can
dig a poncho out of the pack and flap my way down to
shelter—a clump of dwarf spruce, boughs packed as
densely as any bush. I hesitate, but a flash of light and a
roar that shakes the ground drive me to my belly inside.
I toss out the camera gear, my knife, belt, and tripod.

Black clouds boil about the mountains spitting fire.
The air smells of split rock and scorched earth. Small
comfort that some of these trees have been crisped before. Which is more foolhardy, I debate, to stay or bolt?
I bolt.

A dozen lightning flashes later I'm in camp. Everyone's already down. And how did they manage that?
Dean's crying, chilled and frightened, warmed back to
smiles with soup and cocoa. Press says the trail appears
okay. "Didn't you enjoy the storm?" he asks. "Haven't
you ever seen St. Elmo's fire?"

The horses are packed before sunrise. Just in case there
are any more storms, Press wants to be off Marston's
top before noon. A motion I loudly second.

Midmornings Dean has been complaining of hun-
ger; Bill and I feed him toast until he's round as a little
Buddha, then lift him aboard Dan.

Within the first mile we must chop through three
pines that have fallen across the trail. Others we're able
to detour, though at some difficulty, letting the horses
pick their way carefully over and around the tangle of
deadfall. Feeling those great horse muscles working
uphill between my legs, pointed radar ears flicking
back and forth, listening ahead and then behind and
then both directions at once, watching the packhorses
struggle with our loads, I feel an admiration for the
breed I've never felt before.

Marston Pass's eleven-thousand-foot summit is
gained by a dim trail across talus. A great alpine plateau
dotted with snowfields spreads in all directions. A daz-

zling variety of flowers everywhere: phlox, Indian paintbrush, penstemon, mountain dandelion, elephants head, and primrose—bright spots of purple, gold, red, and yellow. Marmots shuttle from sunning rocks to dens at our approach. Pikas whistle from dark harvest holes. A herd of cow elk (we count seventy through the binoculars) grows nervous at our approach, jump to their feet as if of one mind, and trot away.

Many of the Marston's snowfields are gray in color. Press says this is ash left over from Mount Saint Helens eruption. "That summer the whole high country was black."

And how well I remember that day, sitting at home in Livingston, watching television with Dean, when a bulletin interrupted Dorothy on her trip through Oz—Mount Saint Helens had just blasted thirteen hundred feet off its summit. The shock waves leveled forty-four thousand acres of forest. People ten miles away were killed by poisonous gas. As much pumice fell on Spokane as Vesuvius had cast on Pompeii in A.D. 79.

I've never been able to look at these mountains since and not think of the incomprehensible violence from which they came. Many of these peaks are remnants of Eocene volcanoes once towering thousands of feet above us. Successive waves of solidified magma built this plateau. Glaciers gouged these valleys out, watered the pumice, and sent melt running toward the seas.

It was a popular belief in the early nineteenth century, espoused even by none other than John Charles Frémont, that all the major western rivers rose from a common source, some great mothering Rocky Mountain lake. Even Lewis and Clark had speculated that by following the Yellowstone to its head the source of the Rio del Norte (Colorado) would be discovered and New Spain reached within a ten-day march. When Manuel Lisa sent John Colter up the Bighorn he may have asked him to search for Spaniards as well as Indians.

They weren't entirely wrong. Ninety percent of the water flowing in the West's great rivers does come from the Rocky Mountains, and, though not from a common source, five of the West's major river systems head in the mountains within a hundred mile radius of me. To the west, between us and the shadowy needles of the Teton Mountains, lies the marshy plateau giving rise to the Snake River. To the south, in the Wind River Mountains, are the headwaters of the Bighorn and Green rivers. To the northeast, in the Gallatin Range, rise the streams that will eventually form the Missouri. And to the north, in the Absaroka, rises the Yellowstone.

Arteries all, to even greater systems: Green flowing into the Colorado, Snake into the Columbia, Bighorn into the Yellowstone, Yellowstone into the Missouri, Missouri into the Mississippi. Snow of the same winter storms waters three gulfs.

Seven dams break the Missouri's back. Concrete and steel silence Snake River. Water-skiers play on Green River's Flaming Gorge. Salmon climb artificial ladders up the Columbia to spawn. Only a trickle of the Colo-

rado reaches the ocean. Only the Yellowstone remains
free, roaring down out of the Absaroka as clear and
cold and wild as the day it thawed from Pleistocene ice.

The descent is rigorous. Much of the trail has been destroyed by avalanches of snow and ground. Where
there is a trail, it is steep and generously switchbacked.
Here and there the horses have no alternative but to sit
back on their haunches and slide.

When we're halfway down, a boulder breaks loose
above, crashing toward us, hissing and bouncing, show-
ering us with rolling stones. Press's lead packhorse
spooks, plunging off the trail, yanking the lead rope
through his left hand, nearly jerking him from the saddle. The horse stumbles, falls, rolls to its side, hooves
thrashing the air, regains its feet, stands still, trembling,
until Press can dismount and catch it. In the midst of
the action Dan leaves the trail, apparently to seek his
own route. Losing his grip on the saddle horn, Dean
hugs the horse's neck, rocking dangerously each time
Dan shifts his weight. Mounds of talus tumble ahead of
them. But Dan's only pursuing a succulent bit of lu-
pine. Satisfied, he climbs back up the slope, blue flowers
dangling from the corner of his mouth.

We camp in the first stand of pines growing along
the Yellowstone's south fork, a stream two feet wide
running through willows not far from the tent. Yount's
Peak's pyramid shape looms over us, 12,165 feet high;
named for Mountain Harry Yount, a packer for Ferdinand Vandeveer Hayden's 1878 survey.

Press is trying to have the unnamed peak to the east of us, now designated as number 242, christened for his old packing mentor, Jack Davis.

Before World War II, Jack Davis spent his winters gathering wild mules in Arizona, his summers trailing them north to sell in Wyoming. When fences tangled his route, he stayed with the last bunch of mules he sold and went to work for the Teton Valley Ranch in Jackson Hole. Twenty years later, when the Turner family bought the TVR's mules for the Triangle X Ranch, Jack Davis came with the deal. "I stay with the mules," he told them. And stay he did, becoming the wizened wizard of the tack room, sipping medicinal whiskey and smoking that outlandish pipe, admonishing the clumsy not to be a messin' with things they didn't understand. On packtrips he woke boys (Press was one) by stepping lightly on their heads and hollering, "Indians! Indians!" or "Don't get sunburnt in bed!" When he died his ashes were scattered over Yount's Peak.

"Jack Davis never camped low when he could camp high," says Press.

This is how the Yellowstone begins—a dark stain seeping down the flank of Yount's Peak from beneath melting snow. Hundreds of rivulets gathering among the elk dung and tundra flowers. A glimmer of silver through the willow below.

Few trees grow at this altitude. An occasional stunted spruce or whitebark pine clinging to shelter, trunks winter bent, boughs deformed by an almost

15

constant wind. The air is cold and raw in my low-land lungs. Mountains roll away to the horizon in every direction I look, ridge after gray rock ridge set upon blunt Alpine base.

Two thousand feet down, our camp appears an ant-sized island of bright nylon and canvas, smoke from our supper fire putting a slight smudge against cliffs of the Continental Divide, occasional gongs and clanks of the horses' bells rising like fairy notes.

In the snow six inches from my hand is the track of a grizzly.

We hiked up the peak this morning. Ostensibly, our mission was to recover the register Jack Davis left in a mason jar beneath a rock cairn on the summit in 1945. But the register wasn't to be found, and in lieu of signing the original we made our own. Press left a note about Jack Davis. Dean printed his name in big letters and put a 5 beside it. And now, much faster than we came up, we scramble down.

After supper, while doing dishes, I mention the bear track to Press. "There's a fresh dig not far from camp," he says, "some bear trying to get at a marmot. Lord Griz. He's around here, that's for sure."

Mentioning it initiates a round of bear stories—and what Yellowstone night would be complete without them? One night on his first packtrip a grizzly walked between the fire and his tent—that great humped silhouette sliding across canvas. Press spent the night beating on a tin pan with a spoon, bear's eyes glowing at the edge of light. Next morning the horses were gone. None of the dudes had heard a thing.

"We found the horses at Bridger Lake, eight miles away," says Press, "and also some campers in trees where the bear'd put them. Their camp was in ruins. Way out in a meadow was a coffee pot torn in half. Whenever people talk about bears, I see that twisted coffee pot laying pathetically in the grass."

A friend of Jack's had a bear sniff his ear through a tent. A bear once knocked Jack's tent down and sat on his head. "Of course that was a black bear, not a griz," he adds, somewhat apologetically.

Bill's heard that grizzlies are already raiding hunting camps on Falcon Creek.

My favorite campfire bear tale is that of Hugh Glass. Glass was a seaman whose ship was captured by Lafitte. The pirate gave Glass the choice of becoming a brother or sharkbait and Glass made the sensible choice. He escaped overboard one night several years later, swam to Texas, and started walking north. He nearly starved to death on the Kansas plains before some Pawnee captured him. For the next five years he was a slave, but such a good one that he was allowed to accompany a chieftain's delegation to St. Louis. There Glass jumped aboard William Ashley's keelboat bound upriver toward beaver country.

That fall, hunting in advance of the main party, Glass was pounced on by a sow grizzly. He got off his one shot, and was then, in the words of a witness, "tore nearly all to peases." Glass was expected to die, and Ashley, pressed by Indian danger, left him behind with two caretakers, supposedly young James Bridger and

Tom Fitzgerald, whom he induced to stay with promise of extra pay. But the pair stayed only until their fear and the certainty of Glass's dying got the better of them. They fled, taking Glass's rifle and all his accoutrements, and reported his demise.

But Hugh Glass was a tenacious man and having overheard what had transpired, vowed he'd live to collect revenge. For a time he lived on his back beneath a cutbank within an arm's reach of water and overhanging berries. He stoned a rattlesnake to death and mashed its flesh into a broth. When he was strong enough, he started crawling in the direction of Fort Hall on the Missouri, three hundred miles away. Flies laid eggs in festering wounds he couldn't reach. Buzzards and magpies haunted his progress. He lived on wolf kills, anything he could catch. At an abandoned Indian village he killed a dog. Soon, he could walk.

At Fort Hall he learned that his men and precious rifle were at the Yellowstone's mouth. After staying less than a week he set off after them in the company of five trappers going upriver to winter in the Mandan villages. Impatience with the Missouri's slow bends overtook Glass six weeks into the journey and he asked to be put ashore. That night his companions were ambushed and killed by Arikaras, Glass within hearing distance of their screams. When he arrived at the Yellowstone's mouth a month later, he found the post abandoned; the men he wanted were at Fort Cass, three hundred miles upriver at the Bighorn's mouth, the site of Manuel Lisa's old post.

Glass arrived at Fort Cass on Christmas Eve night.

Fitzgerald had lost his taste for the wilderness and gone south to join the army at Fort Atkinson, Kansas, and had taken Glass's rifle with him. But what transpired within the two minds as their eyes met, each thinking the other dead, when Glass confronted Bridger. Bridger was only seventeen. Glass wouldn't take his revenge on a kid.

"You've been on borrowed time," Glass is supposed to have said, "you've not known it, but your life's been mine. Now I give it back. Do with it what you will. Make good or throw it away. I forgive you, but will God?"

Two months later Glass was on his way south.

He would have killed Fitzgerald when he found him but the commander wouldn't permit it. He did get his rifle back, the same he was carrying nine years later when the Arikara caught him on the Yellowstone ice below Fort Cass and put an end to his time.

At dawn, as soon as the pancakes and eggs are eaten, as we're weighing out our respective loads, sorting last moment equipment—two camera bodies or three? The 28mm lens or the 24mm? Do we really need all that cocoa?—it begins to rain. An hour later the rain has turned to snow.

"If God had meant for man to carry loads he would have given him four legs, not two," Press says. "That's what horses are for."

We shake hands all around, give Dan, Jigs, and Kitty a last pat on the neck—they're going to be sorely missed. Jack, Bill, and Press mount up, splash across the

Yellowstone, and dissolve into the storm. For long minutes afterwards we hear faint echoes of their movement, a snatch of conversation and laughter, a bar or two of one of Jack's sad songs, a horse blowing, a bough brushing canvas, and then silence. Alone.

Shouldering packs, we begin walking west on an elk trail of bent grass beside the Yellowstone. I lead, feeling the complaint of unconditioned muscles, blades of pain in my shoulders and back, the pinch of fat between Levi's and waistbelt.

Dean follows, bundled in his capote, carrying our lunch. Alisa brings up the rear, stopping when Dean stops, stooping to examine snowflakes and animal tracks with him, answering his questions about gnomes, trolls, and bears, and urging him along. The valley is a quarter mile across, rocky slopes leading up to cliffs on either side. Visibility is so poor that we spend most of our time walking heads down.

Within a mile we jump across the river and enter a lodgepole forest. Somber, quiet country. A vague trail; deadfall lies across our path in tiers two and three trees deep, like matchsticks tossed from a giant's box. Red breccia walls on either side grow steeper, banded by ledges and an occasional dark stain of pine, pockmarked by the cooling and bursting of hot magma bubbles. Waterfalls pour down their faces in quicksilver cords, rush across our path, swelling the Yellowstone to a roar.

In the afternoon we leave the timber for a long narrow meadow strewn with house-sized boulders, conglomerates bound to each other by the hot cement of creation. Avalanches of smaller rocks have poured down off the cliffs and fanned out into the grass. The valley's hard lines are softened by eight inches of snow, grass and willows and tree boughs bent, deadfall and rocks hidden in white lumps. There are tracks of mice and snowshoe hare; great dark holes punched by moose. Blue-black storm clouds obscure the mountains, but we feel their presence all around. Our heartbeats and breathing are the only sounds; even the river, flowing through the valley's center, is silent, backed up in ponds behind beaver dams. It's as if the Pleistocene ice has just withdrawn, leaving a primeval Eden, raw and unfinished.

A mile further, and we succumb to temptation and make an early camp, pitching the tent in a narrow fringe of timber at a cliff base on the valley's northwest edge.

I clump off to fetch water, filling our canvas bags in a pool beneath a waterfall roaring a thousand feet down off the Continental Divide, water so fresh from snow that drinking it sends sharp pains to my temples, yet so delicious, so intoxicating, I can't drink enough. On my way back, poking about among the rocks, I find a stick figure etched on the sheltered side of a boulder, arms outstretched, moon face staring at me—some other consciousness, some other thought, snapping from cold stone into my fingertips. What was your name for this place, I wonder, and how did it sound in your tongue? How strange to think that the two of us exist in this valley almost within the same creative sigh.

Over the mountain stove's intermittent blue flame

we hiccup freeze-dried beans and weenies, eat standing up around a fire.

After we're finished with the dishes, we look about for a tree to hang the food and packs out of bruin's reach during the night; nothing here is done without consideration for Griz, without wondering where he is, where he might be, or when he might pass through.

A stout pine, well away from camp, is selected. I tie nylon cord around a rock and throw it over a bough. A feat much easier to describe than accomplish, taking me a half-dozen throws and as many rocks. We tie the cord to the pack frames, cover the packs with a poncho, and hoist them aloft.

Soon after we're settled into our bags a boulder breaks loose from the cliff above and crashes into the timber, driving a tree down in an explosion of splintering boughs. Rocks continue to fall at intervals all night, some landing in the meadow with thuds, others seeming to crash toward us as if deliberately thrown.

I sleep fitfully: rocks falling, tree trunks skreeking, wind rattling the tent. Listening. Listening.

A sound—what?—a footstep?—snaps my eyes open. It's still dark outside. I dress as quietly as I can, as much in the sleeping bag as possible, trying not to bump the tent's drooping sides, breath coming out in clouds. Spoil it all by breaking a frozen bootlace and waking the family with a curse.

"What's the matter?" Alisa asks.

I touch a finger to her lips: "Shhhh."

But the sound doesn't repeat.

I've barely drifted back to sleep when a loud snort makes all of us sit up in unison. Alisa and I speculate hurriedly in whispers. I slowly unzip the tent door until I can peek through a crack. A hairy pair of knees ten yards away. A wary bull moose watching me, freshly shorn velvet hanging in bloody strips from white antlers. The bull belches, shakes his head, velvet fluttering like rags, dangling bell of fur flopping side to side beneath his chin, breath coming out in twin smoky jets. "Go on," I say in a voice as calm as I can muster, "get the hell out of here." No effect. A second bull moose strolls out of the woods passing within a stone's toss of the tent. The duo confront us, dumbfounded. Some new wonder! Should we give it a poke? Moose number one wipes his antlers through a small pine tree, bending it until it breaks. The two begin shoving each other back and forth, playfully, white antler clacking upon white antler like castanets. I steal out of the tent and over to the ashes of last night's fire, huffing until the coals glow, throwing on tinder. The bulls disengage and approach, snuffling for the scent.

"Fire!" I say whirling around, thrusting out a smoldering stick. "Man!" The bulls act as if I'm offering something to eat, purse their lips for a nibble, reconsider, ruminate, then wheel and trot away, first day's light rippling across their black backs.

The snow melts even as we pack. Wet grass soaks us to the knees before we've traveled a hundred yards, but we bask in the warmth. "Oh, thank you sun," says

Dean. At the meadow's north end we cross the Yellowstone on the slick backs of four round stones and enter
a lush forest of pine, spruce, and fir. Snow dropping
from boughs surrounds us with a fine diamond mist.
Droplets of water glisten on fern leaves, berry bushes,
and flowers. *Agaricus* mushrooms the size of bread
loaves grow beside the trail. The ground is soft with
pine needles and small cones. We lose the trail often in
deadfall, cast about like hounds, find it, walk a short
way, and lose it again. Lynx tracks in the mud, also deer,
elk, and moose. Every now and then a black bear print.
Logs lying across the way have been polished smooth
by numerous undersides, all kinds of long hairs caught
on splinters.

The Yellowstone tumbles down through pale lichen-
stained boulders in a small canyon on our left. We wade
across a dozen small streams in the course of an hour,
all unnamed, none of them on the map.

At noon we take a last look back at Yount's Peak,
snow blowing in wind-driven banners from its summit.
Still winter up there. We've dropped two thousand feet
since breaking camp, moving steadily down from forest
to meadow, meadow to forest.

A mile further and the Yellowstone's south fork is
joined by its north. We must walk upstream a mile to
find a ford, as the water is swollen and brown with melt.
Using sticks for wading staffs we cross three abreast,
holding hands, Dean between Alisa and me, moving
one step at a time, fast water pressing against our legs,
all of us hooting at the cold.

In the afternoon we make another early camp, pitching the tent on a gravel island midstream. Progress with Dean is slow, but Alisa's and my muscles are sore, and speed isn't our object anyway.

While scouring the supper dishes with sand, I find grizzly tracks on the beach. Alisa and I stay up late, feeding the fire with driftwood, drinking tea, counting falling stars in the moonless sky, listening to the stream. I am uneasy. Thoughts of bear crowd my mind, a fear growing larger and colder with the night.

When I was thirteen a former Alaskan policeman showed me photographs of two bear hunters a grizzly had killed. The bear's tracks had paralleled theirs from the moment they'd left their floatplane. When they'd stopped to smoke, the bear had lain in the willows and waited. One's arms were frozen as if still holding a rifle, the bloody snow around him littered with spent cartridges, great dime-sized tooth holes in his head, the rifle, stock smashed, barrel bent, lying at his side. The other man had no head. The ground looked as if a bulldozer had been at work.

Tonight those images play through my mind like a macabre black-and-white slide show. Grizzly.

Two Octobers ago a friend and I heard that a sow grizzly was feeding on a buffalo carcass near an old dump in Yellowstone Park. The buffalo had been killed on the highway by a car and carried to the dump by a front-end loader. The bear could be seen from a car if that car passed through the locked gate of a service road. My friend had a key. That first evening a half dozen other cars were parked in front of the carcass. It was like waiting for a drive-in movie to begin. But gradually, as the occupants bored, the other cars left until there was just my friend and I, sitting in his jeep, in the dark, listening to elk bugle, and enjoying the autumn chill. We could hear mice rustling in the grass, the soft passage of owls overhead. The buffalo was thirty yards away. Our plan was to hit the lights when we heard the grizzly feeding. All we wanted was a glimpse. We waited an hour before deciding to go. Started the motor and turned on the headlights—and there she was, already covering the carcass. Then she was gone.

We returned at dawn, but she wasn't around. We tried again at noon, not expecting her at all, and there she was—tugging at a bison leg, watching us like a dog worrying a bone. She was blonde, head and legs running to black, a silver raccoon mask across her eyes. The sow reared up, ivory claws hanging down, nose upthrust, body swaying, breath coming out in frosty huffs—dropped to the ground and began rocking from her front feet to her back, so rapidly she appeared to be bouncing. She charged soundlessly. The jeep wouldn't start. Bracing myself against the door I wondered how bad it would be. But the sow veered at ten feet, spewing gravel on us, and loped into the lodgepoles on the other side.

And sometimes when I think of grizzlies it's her teeth and claws that I see, the sudden death in those eyes, how silently and unpredictably it can materialize.

· · ·

Coyotes howl at our fire from caves in the cliffs, a mad echoing laughter that haunts sleep.

Before dawn the river reflects stars in its pools, the woods shapeless, mountains only hints of form. I scan it all slowly, turning my head an inch at a time, straining to see. Nothing moves.

A half hour later the night's fears are taken away by the sun. The pool below camp produces four cutthroat trout for breakfast: eaten parboiled with a light shake of salt. The river drops through a large canyon, water so clear we can see trout trembling against sand in the pools, golden ripples of light passing over the bottom. Dean walks in the lead today asking questions constantly. Why do rocks fall? What makes flowers different? What track is this? Where do animals sleep? We the explainers become enchanted in the answering.

We pass Castle Creek (for the shape of the peak on the eastern horizon), the first named tributary entering the Yellowstone. Thorofare Valley opens up before us, a mile wide, willows stretching north for as far as we can see. Flocks of ducks wheel out over the river, wings flashing in sunlight. Goose families tune up their honks. A cow moose glides across our path. Three blue grouse cluck out of way like chickens.

The further we walk the wider the valley becomes, until at last even the trail leaves timber and plunges into willow, becoming a muddy moose road of tracks and dung, secret moose passageways branching off to the sides. The willows are over our heads, so thick we can see only a few feet ahead. No telling around which bend we'll have to give right of way to a moose. Or worse. Mosquitoes and deerflies hum in front of our faces. For the first time on the trip we're too warm and strip to T-shirts.

Finally Dean can be induced no farther with promises of the sand castle beaches awaiting us at Bridger Lake. At sunset we put down in an island of pine trees not far from the Hawk's Rest Ranger Station, usually manned though not tonight.

There is a story about a fireguard who brought his bride to Hawk's Rest for a summer of honeymooning. The first night a bear came crashing through a window onto the bed. The fireguard's new wife helicoptered out the next day.

Our campsite destroys any illusion of wilderness we might have entertained. All the pine branches within arm's reach have been stripped for firewood. Tree trunks have been girdled by gnawing pack animals. Toilet paper in the brush. Rusty cans litter the ground. Garbage has been dug up and scattered by coyotes and bears. We have an infinite choice of charred fire rings. It's too dark to move on so we pitch the tent with its door, one side, and rear facing trees, flank the open side with a fire, just in case a trash-mongering grizzly happens by.

Oddly quiet. We're without the sound of moving water tonight. There's no wind. We sleep on top of our bags while geese talk restlessly in the willows all night.

· · ·

This morning we decide to hike a mile and breakfast at Bridger Lake rather than stay about the dump. The trail isn't hard to follow, a half dozen ruts. Many official wooden signs give us the mileage and point the way. No wonder it's named the Thorofare.

We cross the Yellowstone on a frosted log bridge. The river is two hundred feet across, surprisingly slow and deep. Until we're warmed up by walking we wear wool shirts.

Much to Dean's disappointment and my chagrin, Bridger Lake has no sand beaches. Lodgepole and deadfall are right up to the water. The lake's named for James Bridger, who came into the Yellowstone country with Ashley and Henry in 1822 as one of the Rocky Mountain Fur Company's ambitious young men. Old Gabe—roamer, loner, and storyteller extraordinaire. Once Bridger didn't eat bread for seventeen years. He was the first white man to see the Great Salt Lake (he thought it an inland arm of the Pacific), discovered South Pass, and founded the Oregon Trail. The West was mapped more accurately in Bridger's mind than it was in print. At the age of fifty he built his own fort, became a trader, interpreter, counselor, and guide.

In 1859 Captain William Raynolds of the Topographical Engineers, along with an astronomer, topographer, geologist, meteorologist, naturalist, thirty infantry, an odometer, and sixty-four mule-drawn carts, set off from Fort Pierre, South Dakota—one of their missions to find a route from South Pass across the Yellowstone's headwaters to the Missouri. Ferdinand

Vandavier Hayden was the naturalist, James Bridger the guide.

During the expedition's six tedious months in winter quarters on the Upper Platte, Raynolds listened to the Yellowstone tales of his "American guide."

Bridger spared Raynolds few of his imaginative gems, and the good captain, thinking these "Münchhausen tales" too good to be lost, wrote them down.

"One was to this effect: in parts of the country petrifications and fossil are numerous. As a consequence, in a certain locality, a large tract of sage is petrified, its leaves and branches all stone, while the rabbits and sage hens are still there, all perfectly petrified . . . more wonderful still, these petrified bushes bear diamonds, rubies, sapphires, and emeralds, some as large as walnuts.

"Another story: a party of whites was pursued by the Indians, the enemy being so close the whites were forced to hide during the day and travel only at night; but in this they were aided by a huge diamond on the face of a neighboring mountain, by the light of which they traveled for three nights.

"In one of his recitals [Bridger] described an immense boiling spring that is perfect counter-part of the Geysers of Iceland. As he is uneducated, and had probably never heard of the existence of such natural marvels elsewhere, I have little doubt that he spoke of that which he had actually seen.

"Bridger also insisted that . . . there is a stream of considerable size which divides, and flows down either side of the water shed, thus discharging its waters into both the Atlantic and Pacific Oceans."

When spring came Raynolds was determined to see what part of these tales was based in truth. Bridger warned him he couldn't cross the Absaroka. But the captain insisted and a week later penned, "Directly across our route lies a basaltic ridge, rising not less than 5,000 feet above us, its wall apparently vertical with no visible pass nor even cañon. . . . On the opposite side of this are the headwaters of the Yellowstone. Bridger remarked triumphantly and forcibly to me upon reaching this spot: 'I told you you could not go through. A bird can't fly over that without taking a supply of grub along.' I had no reply to offer, and mentally conceded the accuracy of the information of 'the old man of the mountains.'"

Raynolds tried to gain the Yellowstone's headwaters one more time, but the men and animals mired in the spring thaw. On June 4 Raynolds wrote of "a spirit of insubordination and discontent manifest among the men showing itself openly in their apparent determination to abandon the odometer wheels." On June 5 he counted "twenty-five mules plunged deep in the mud, totally unable to extricate themselves."

"The valley of the Upper Yellowstone is yet a terra-incognita," he wrote, "and we were compelled to content ourselves with listening to marvelous tales of burning plains, immense lakes, and boiling springs, without being able to verify these wonders."

Though John Colter had probably seen something of the Upper Yellowstone in 1807 and James Bridger certainly had by 1835, along with a few score of others, red and white, nowhere is the lack of official recognition more apparent than in the map Raynolds included with his report: five thousand square miles of blank space rimmed by impenetrable mountains—an island of wild amid a settled sea. It was almost as if the Absaroka guarded the Yellowstone, waiting for the right men to seek it.

We skirt Bridger Lake's south shore, passing through dense stands of lodgepole pine. A bald eagle coasts overhead and lands in a snag. A pair of trumpeter swans glide to the lake's center trailed by their gray cygnet brood.

In the muddy trail are fresh grizzly prints. My hiking boot fits within the rear track, slashes six inches out in front of my toes. As we walk I imagine the bear moving ahead of us, great head wagging from side to side, coat rippling over the muscles of shoulder and hump, stopping occasionally to test for scents with upthrust nose, turning over rocks in search of bugs, poking beneath logs, grazing or sleeping or scratching.

"Bears are made of the same dust as we and breathe the same winds and drink of the same waters," John Muir wrote after a Yellowstone tour in 1898, "his life not long, not short, knows no beginning, no ending, to him life unstinted, unplanned is above the accident of time, and his years, markless, boundless, equal eternity."

We're welcomed into Yellowstone Park by a wooden sign. The bear's tracks veer abruptly off the trail. Jim Bridger was fond of telling emigrants, "When you see tracks look out. When you don't see tracks really look out." We move slowly, really looking out. Every so often I stop to test the air with my own inefficient nose, cup my hands around ears to accentuate sound, searching for clues.

By the late 1860s interest in the Upper Yellowstone experienced a renaissance in the form of gold, as all the disappointed forty-niners and those who'd always thought they'd been born too late struck out for the Montana ore fields. Essentially, Yellowstone was discovered by prospectors.

"A portion of the Bear Gulch stampeders have been to the Lake at the head of the Yellowstone," wrote the *Montana Post*'s editor on August 31, 1867, "and report the greatest wonder of the age. For eight days they traveled through a volcanic country emitting blue flames, living streams of molten brimstone, and almost every variety of minerals known to chemists. . . . The steam and blaze was constantly discharging from these subterranean channels in regular evolutions of exhaustions, like the boilers of our steam boats, and gave the same roaring, whistling sound. . . . Mr. Hubel, who has visited this region before, ventured to approach one of the smaller ones.

"As he neared its mouth his feet broke through and the blue flame and smoke gushed forth, enveloping him. Dropping upon his body, he crawled to within a couple of feet of the crater and saw that the crust around its edge was thin like a wafer. Lighting a match he extended it to the mouth and instantly it was on fire. . . . On their return they encountered four men on four splendid American horses, driving thirty-six large mules, in fine condition, all branded 'U.S.' Said individuals wore linen dusters and heavy gold rings on their fingers—traveled southward—understood the country—acted suspiciously, and that's all that's known."

By far the most well-known miners' excursion into Yellowstone is that of Charles Cook, William Peterson, and David E. Folsom who departed Diamond City, Montana Territory, in the autumn of 1869 and returned, overwhelmed, twenty-one days later. They'd seen truths that put Bridger's tales to shame.

Years later Cook recalled that he and his partners talked of how the country that they had seen would soon be in private hands and though "none of us definitely suggested the idea of a national park . . . we knew that as soon as the wonderful character of the country was generally known outside, there would be plenty of people hurrying in to get possession, unless something was done."

The respectable press—*Scribner's Magazine* and the *New York Tribune*—refused to publish an account of Cook's journey because of a "reputation they could not risk." An edited version of Cook's journal did appear in *Western Monthly* magazine, inspiring the first official exploration of the Upper Yellowstone by an unlikely and uninspiring band of Montana Territory army officers, politicians, merchants, and lawyers, among them: General Henry Dana Washburn, surveyor-general, who'd marched with Sherman through Georgia; Nathaniel P. Langford, ex-vigilante and tax collector; Cornelius Hedges, future U.S. district attorney; and Truman C. Evert, assessor of internal revenue.

Leaving Fort Ellis, near present-day Bozeman, Montana, the following spring—complete with cavalry escort under command of Lieutenant Gustavus C. Doane, rations for thirty days, and a dog named Booby—they proceeded east over Bozeman Pass and turned south up the Yellowstone.

Two weeks later they sat around a hotsprings by the Madison River contemplating what to do with all they'd witnessed. According to Langford's journal:

> The proposition was made by some member that we utilize the result of our exploration by taking up quarter sections of land at the most prominent points of interest, and a general discussion followed. One member of our party suggested that if there could be secured by preemption a good title to two or three quarter sections of land opposite the [Yellowstone's] Lower Falls and extending down the river along the canyon, they would eventually become a source of great profit to the owners. Another member of the party thought that it would be more desirable to take up a quarter section of land at the Upper Geyser Basin, for the reason that the locality could be more easily reached by tourists and pleasure seekers. A third suggestion was that each member of the party preempt a claim, and in order that

no one should have an advantage over the others, the whole would be thrown into a common pool for the benefit of the entire party. Mr. Hedges then said that he did not approve of any of these plans—that there ought to be no private ownership of any portion of that region, but the whole ought to be set apart as a great National Park, and that each one of us ought to make an effort to have this accomplished.

That winter, financed by the Northern Pacific Railroad tycoon, Jay Cooke, Nathaniel Langford lectured in the East and wrote magazine articles.

Ferdinand Vandavier Hayden, now the illustrious wunderkind director of the Geological and Geographical Society of the Territories, and no doubt remembering Bridger's camp tales, listened to a Langford lecture and opted to launch a Yellowstone Survey instead of spending another summer in the Dakotas among hostile Sioux. Congress appropriated $40,000 for the venture.

During the Civil War Hayden had served as a surgeon, and it had nearly driven him mad. After the war he spent two years wandering alone over the Dakotas picking up fossils, tapping rocks, evolving theories of how the continents were formed and what lay underneath. The Indians called him Man Who Picks Up Stones Running.

Hayden believed it his duty to locate and classify the West's resources, thus pointing the way for efficient use of the country—a businessman's geologist. By 1869 he'd founded and become sole employee of The Geological Survey of the Territories.

Hayden realized that only widespread public support would keep his survey alive by keeping congressional appropriations flowing. Thus he sought popular appeal. By using photography and illustrations in his reports, Hayden found a way of documenting the West as well as presenting it artistically.

William H. Jackson had fled Pennsylvania because of thwarted love and came west as a bullwhacker, "the severest physical hardship I have ever known." In Omaha he started a photography business with his brother Ed, doing "portrait jobs; group pictures of lodges, church societies, and political clubs; and outdoor shots that gratified civic pride . . . shop fronts and, occasionally, interiors. Now and then, too, somebody would order pictures of his new house; or of his big barn, and along with it the livestock."

Jackson was working for the Northern Pacific Railroad, shooting views of the new western routes, when he met Hayden, who, impressed by his photography, offered him "a summer of hard work—and the satisfaction . . . you would find in contributing your art to science." Jackson sold his share of the studio to Ed, shipped his bride to her folks, and joined the survey.

Thomas Moran had immigrated to the United States from England with his parents when he was seven. His brothers Edward and Peter were painters; his brother John a photographer. Thomas became an engraver at the age of eighteen, occasionally selling a watercolor portrait on the side. After engraving for two years, he "left it to begin the practice of Art without a master."

Now and then he took engraving work to pay the bills. It was he who rendered Langford's descriptions into drawings for "The Wonders of Yellowstone," published in the December 1871 *Scribner's Magazine*. Inspired by the strange landscape of Yellowstone, Moran appealed to Jay Cooke to outfit him for a trip. Cooke did better than that, he introduced Moran to Hayden.

Before joining the Hayden expedition, Moran had been no further west than the Hudson. "He was as poorly equipped for rough life as anyone I have ever known," William H. Jackson wrote in his memoirs. "Never had he mounted a horse and then he did so with a pillow tucked in over the cantle of his saddle. Frail, almost cadaverous, he seemed incapable of surviving the rigors of camp life and camp food."

"You should see me bolt the bacon," Moran wrote in a letter to a friend.

The Hayden expedition left Fort Ellis on July 15, 1871. It included twenty associates, visitors, and guests, among them an agricultural statistician, three topographers, a meteorologist, botanist, minerologist, and a zoologist. At Bottler's Ranch on the Yellowstone, the survey exchanged wagons for packmules and proceeded upriver to the mouth of Gardiner River, discovering Mammoth Hot Springs. From Mammoth, the survey rode east to Tower Creek, passed over the saddle between Mounts Dunraven and Washburn, and dropped swiftly down through the lodgepoles to the

brink of the Yellowstone's Grand Canyon, where Tom
Moran nearly wept for the lack of colors on his palette,
and Jackson, scrambling from one precarious view to
another, made exposure after exposure on his glass
plates. From the canyon the survey rode south through
the valley now bearing Hayden's name. They passed
down the east side of Yellowstone Lake and went
around the southern arms and up the west shore, crossing into the Firehole geyser basin.

"We pass with rapid transition from one remarkable
vision to another," wrote Hayden, "each unique of its
kind and surpassing all others in the known world. The
intelligent American will one day point on the map to
this remarkable district with the conscious pride that it
has not its parallel on the face of the globe."

The expedition returned to Fort Ellis thirty-eight
days later. Hayden hastily compiled a three-hundred-
page report for Congress. Moran turned his studies into
finished paintings and Jackson cranked out prints—
the sum of their efforts introduced Yellowstone to the
world.

On March 1, 1872, President Grant signed into law
"an act to set apart a certain tract of land laying near the
headwaters of the Yellowstone River as a public park
. . . for the benefit and enjoyment of the people. . . ."

The national park idea wasn't new. Forty-four
square miles of Yosemite Valley had been set aside as a
forest reserve just a few years earlier. In 1834 the artist
George Catlin had urged that vast tracts of the Rocky
Mountain west be set aside as ". . . a nation's park, con-

taining man and beast, in all the wild freshness of their nature's beauty!"

And yet Yellowstone Park's creation was an astonishing concept, coming as it did, four years before Custer's death, a decade preceding the annihilation of the northern buffalo herds. It becomes even more remarkable when you consider the difference in what was intended by the park idea and what has transpired. The national park Hedges envisioned consisted of a few fenced acres around the grandest features. When Hayden drew up the new park's boundaries, he included 3,200 square miles to protect as many undiscovered "decorations" as possible. Preserving wildness was the furthest thing from anyone's mind.

A mile past Thorofare Creek (more river than creek), its gravel banks shoved into piles from the spring floods, we arrive at the Thorofare Ranger Station. The Thorofare ranger himself, Bob Jackson, is out back by the woodpile skinning logs for a new porch.

"How's Smokey?" Dean asks.

"Ya didn't run into that griz at Bridger Lake didja?" Bob asks. "He's a big one. Hit a camp just last night, snatched some steaks right off the fire."

The Thorofare cabin was built in 1916. "It's the last of the original Park Service posts," Bob says, "all the others were dismantled, replaced by sleek new A-frames delivered by chopper." Bob Jackson hopes none of that comes to pass here. He likes the old cabin, the backwoods life.

Bob winters on an Iowa farm raising organic tomatoes and buffalo. Come spring he hops in his '52 International pickup and boogies to Yellowstone where he's worked as a seasonal ranger for thirteen summers. He's thirty-three and started out as a fireguard. Now, as a backcountry ranger, or more specifically, the Thorofare Ranger, he's as high up in the government as he aspires, forty miles from paperwork and supervisors.

He rides into the Thorofare the end of June. The streams are still high with runoff then. "You bring your tallest horse," he says. He stays until the winter storms drive him out, like an elk, in November—the lone ranger in a thousand square miles, the only law west of the Trident and east of the Continental Divide, rescuer of the lost, dispenser of information, checker of permits, builder of trails, protector of game.

This morning he found seven freshly poached elk. And somebody had put porcupine quills in his horse corral so that when his horses rolled they'd get a back full of quills—"What kind of demented person would do that?"

His people in Iowa think he walks around with a shovel putting out fires. The other rangers back at headquarters ask him if he doesn't get bored: no lights, no running water, no steak house, no bar, no dudes, no action, no women. Bob Jackson scoffs, says, "I'd come earlier and stay later if I could."

He shows us a muddy paw print on the cabin door. "Griz are always trying to get in the cabins," he says, "especially in the fall, long about now. Griz kept breaking into the Cabin Creek cabin so much the government moved it. Sometimes in the spring I'd find the door of the Cabin Creek cabin hanging open. All the pots and pans and cans and mattresses laying outside. Some mornings prints are in the frost on the porch. Sometimes nights you hear the door creak as if something's testing it. In the Thorofare," he says, "you learn to knock on the door before you go out." He carries a pistol to the john.

"After a month," he says, "your sense of smell improves. Your eyesight and hearing get better. You become attuned. Laying down on your belly to get a drink of water you look around, check things out just like an animal. You get wary. Without griz, without the fear, that awareness that the bear brings, Yellowstone would just be another postcard-pretty park. It's the griz that keeps it wild."

When he used to be a patrolman in the Pelican Valley, the park's premiere bear habitat, he would see twenty grizzlies a week. "Now," he says, "with all the hikers in the Pelican, you're lucky to see sign."

He was charged by a grizzly once. His best friend's wife was mauled not far from the Lake Ranger Station. "It's one of the risks."

As he brews coffee, ranger-style, boiled on the wood stove, Bob shows us the cabin's log, the daily record kept by rangers since the cabin was built. A few excerpts:

8/14/69
Got a surprise last night. At around 2200 I went outside to brush teeth, check stars, etc., in preparation

to go to bed and almost ran into a griz. As I stepped out from light to darkness he snorted and blew and left and I did same in opposite direction only faster. Didn't see him just heard him. Must have been about hitch rack distance where the first little trees are. But enough to make me shine the light around next time out.

9/5/73
0430 Awakened by the screen door swinging and the top screen being ripped followed by the front door creaking as if something were leaning in or pushing on it (something big). Activity then ceased, left front door and began at southeast kitchen window, smashed in screen and all, during commotion I got up, was reaching for the flashlight then gun, shouting, cursing in ever increasing volume. It sounded as if something landed on the kitchen floor. Ten minutes later a mouse sprang one of the mousetraps. That mousetrap must have had one of the most startling effects in history. Broad daylight checked for tracks, found only a few, coming in from the crick. They measured ten inches from tip of hind toe to heel.

9/6/73
Spent an unsettling night waiting for another encounter. Nothing happened.

"One night when I was a fireguard at Lake," Bob interrupts our reading to say, "I walked out of the office to look around, shut the door and stepped forward only to realize that there was a sow grizzly at the trash cans ten yards away. I reached back to open the door but it'd locked behind me. The bear started advancing toward me, very slowly, one step at a time while I frantically searched my pockets for the keys. When the door opened and the light from inside hit her she whirled and left. I still wonder if she was curious or meant harm."

8/20/40
Eight visitors to Thorofare cabin. All women in a pack outfit from the A-A dude ranch in Wyoming (two too young, two too old, but overall not a bad bunch).

8/21/40 "Ranger Services":
Yesterday evening and a good share of the night was spent at Bridger Lake at dinner and playing cards with the ladies at camp there. A good time was had by all. Curbby was the chief entertainer with his (nicer) group of stories.

10/8/40
Strum proved undoubtedly he was the toughest man in Thorofare by falling off the roof three times today, and hitting a pole fence and not receiving a scratch. But oh the language.

10/10/40
Curbby and Strum returned to the old homestead in a downpour of rain.

10/11/40

Curbby and Strum rode to the top of the Trident today and took some pictures. Certainly an excellent
view from up there. A hard ride though. After coming off the Trident went to check on an outfitter
from the Elkhorn Ranch at Bridger Lake. On the
trail home Curbby and I saw a most spectacular
sight, down in the lake cute dude girls were bathing.
We rode right onto them before we saw them and
I'm afraid we were not too modest in our laughing.
In fact it was fortunate that I carried a lariat as I
caught Curbby by the hind legs as he reached the
shore. The girls gave off the usual modest screams
and scrambled for articles of clothing. After con-
trolling Curbby we rode on home, however Curbby
bellowed and pawed the whole way. No doubt he
has been out here too long.

Bob Jackson offers supper, a floor for the night, and
a solar shower under his fifty-gallon barrel, but we decline. It's four miles through the willows to our designated camp and the shadows are getting long. He walks
us out to the creek where he gets his water and promises
to catch up with us tomorrow and show us an Indian
campsite. "But just in case I don't see ya ever again," he
says thrusting out his hand, grinning, "have a nice life."
We leave him standing alone, in his blue jeans, moccasins, and gray shirt, watching the sun go down behind
the Two Ocean Plateau.

We camp in a finger of pine jutting into a meadow

on a wide Yellowstone curve. Grass and willow extend toward dark brooding mountains in every direction. After we pitch the tent, hang the packs, and finish supper, Alisa sets off up the beach to fish, pants rolled to her knees, fly rod in hand, Dean behind, dragging a stick.

Sitting in the warm sand I watch cow elk graze down out of the aspen on the hills to the east. Bulls bugle in the timber, high, broken whistles floating back and forth—the beginning of the rut. A fingerling trout streaks through a still pool, a big trout in pursuit. An osprey plunges into the river, flies away shrieking into twilight, the dark trembling silhouette of a fish in its talons. Off in the brush a moose coughs, a deep guttural uhh. Uhhh. Uhhh.

We linger in camp this morning, taking our time cooking and eating breakfast by the river. Four cow moose browse in willows on the other side. We strip for a swim, dry off, and then begin walking. Fresh bear sign on the trail—big orange piles and tracks.

I knew a man in Colorado who had a dog that would strike a bear's scent and trail it back to where it'd come from, not to where it was going. He said that was either the smartest or the stupidest dog he'd ever raised.

It's hot and dusty. We alternate between lodgepole forest and sagebrush meadow, sunshine and shadow. At the Thorofare's edge, river lost in willows; to the east, our right, rocky Absaroka foothills lead up to peaks. There are bridges across the bogs, trail signs at every intersection. Orange metal tabs hammered into trees keep us from straying from the rutted path.

At Cliff Creek, we encounter our first fellow travelers, a group of backpackers, four men and four women, struggling along between guides. We stand aside. They pass in silence as if somehow acknowledging our presence detracts from their wilderness experience.

In the afternoon we enter forest, and the Yellowstone enters a savannah-like delta of yellow marsh grass, soon to meet the southeastern arm of Yellowstone Lake. Dense stands of lodgepole grow on either side of us, the trail cushioned by pine needles. Deadfall makes a jungle of what little open ground exists. Here and there a fallen tree rots to dust where it lies, a century of growth and slow decay transformed into a shadow of bright green grass. Ravens and jays argue over our progress. Pine squirrels drop cones out of boughs onto soft earth. Every mile, more of the same.

Dean announces that he is a woodsman from Oz. "So you're made of metal, huh?" I say.

"No," says Dean, "that was my brother who rusted."

We cross Cabin Creek. In 1936 three grizzlies tried to dig through the roof of the Cabin Creek patrol cabin. The ranger inside held them at bay with a pitchfork until dawn, giving a poke to every bear that came through the hole.

Another mile (or is it a few), brings us to Beaverdam Creek's willow-filled meadow. In the cool of a dark wood, with shafts of sunlight streaming through boughs, we lunch beside a spring trickling from green moss into a pool, waiting for a bull moose to browse out of the way. In front of us to the north is Yellowstone Lake: the largest, highest freshwater lake on the conti-

47

nent—132 square miles of blue. Gulls wheel overhead. Flocks of ducks wheel above the delta.

The Yellowstone Plateau, which includes much of what we call Yellowstone Park, was formed by a series of volcanic eruptions. The last of these occurred 600,000 years ago when a hot bubble of earth some sixty miles in diameter exploded, leaving a mile-deep hole. Though lesser eruptions built the crater up from within, the lake still marks the caldera's heart.

Eighty thousand years ago, when the lake's shore was three hundred feet higher than it is now, it drained south into the Snake River, but a great change shifted its outlet to the north, into the Yellowstone.

"How can I sum up its wonderful attraction!" wrote Nathaniel Langford of the lake. "It is dotted with islands of great beauty, as yet unvisited by man, but which at no remote period will be adorned with villas and the ornaments of civilized life. [The lake] . . . possesses adaptabilities for the highest display of artificial culture, amid the greatest wonders of Nature that the world affords . . . not many years will elapse before the march of civil improvements will reclaim this delightful solitude, and garnish it with all the attractions of cultivated taste and refinement."

It is interesting to note that while Langford was waxing poetic about the wilderness, another member of the party, poor Truman Everts, Montana's tax assessor, was lost in it. While exploring the lake's southern arm, Everts became separated from the party. His horse shied and ran away, taking Everts's blankets, galoshes, matches, and pistols, leaving him only a penknife. In the morning there was eight inches of snow. His fellow expeditioneers searched the vicinity briefly and then pushed on, thinking Everts would eventually catch up. A month later, the friends were at home by the hearth, basking in the glory of attention. Everts in the meantime had broken his eyeglasses, leaving him nearly blind, had been burned and frostbitten, and had spent a night in a tree with a mountain lion yowling and thumping its tail at the base. His food had been bark and birds and thistle and bugs.

His friends put up a $600 bounty for his return.

Jack Baronett found him on October 6, thirty miles north of where he'd gotten lost.

"My first impulse was to shoot him from where I stood," recalled Baronett. He thought Everts a bear. "I went up close to the object; it was making a low groaning noise, crawling upon its knees and elbows and trying to drag itself up the mountain."

Baronett was turned down when he tried to claim the bounty because he'd found Everts alive. Attempts to claim the money from Everts, and the recovered man's subsequent rudeness, caused Baronett to remark later that he wished he'd let the son of a gun roam.

A huge orange metal sign that warns motorboaters to cut their engines, three wooden picnic tables, and two plastic johns herald our return to civilization at Beaverdam Creek's mouth.

Though this is our designated camping place, Alisa
refuses to sleep here and we walk a mile further, bush-
wack down through deadfall, and pitch the tent in a
grassy spot above the lake. We fall asleep listening to
waves crash against shore.

I walk to the beach for sunrise. The lake is so calm and
smooth that I can see the ring of a trout's rise a quarter
mile out. A veil of steam a few inches high rises from
the surface. I sit still as a stone in the gravel, among the
driftwood and bits of pine needles, the gull feathers and
sand and dried water plants, the small pieces of bone
washed onto the shore. Yellow light breaks through the
pines and touches the water. For an instant, light and
dark, cold and warmth, hang in balance. No sound.
Nothing moves. A gull cries. Air currents rush down
off the mountains and through the pinetops, sweeping
away mist. Day begins.

Elk bugle in the timber. Not often. One here, one
over there. Ravens, waking up, coo and croak and ruffle
their feathers. Jays begin their ceaseless war with squirrels. Sticks snap. A moose grunts. A flock of mallard
ducks chuckle by. "Hello," I say, and they veer off like
fighters. An osprey coasts along the shore, so unaware
of me it passes almost close enough to touch. Golden-
eyes whistle overhead. Mergansers.

Then comes Alisa, walking along the shore picking
up rocks, considering them, and tossing them into the
water to be washed up again in another few centuries.
She sits down beside me to warm in the sun.

We build a fire, make coffee, and drink it with our

backs propped against a log, the sand and gravel forming to our bodies better than any chair, looking out to
the lake.

When Dean wakes we take a plunge, jumping in and
out, shouting, never getting used to the cold, experienc-
ing the same raw shock every time.

Even on the hottest summer day the lake warms to
no more than 52 degrees. A person's life expectancy in
it is about fifteen minutes. In 1971 seven Boy Scouts attempted to cross the southeastern arm during a storm
in canoes. They capsized, and all but one drowned or
succumbed to the cold. The survivor clambered ashore
and began walking north, toward the Park Point patrol
cabin. He was treed by a grizzly that night and died of
exposure the next day.

We wash our clothes, hang them to dry on tree
branches, and spend the remainder of the day wandering up and down the beach like savages, until the chill
drives us back into clothes. Over supper we watch the
lake turn pink and then gold. A loon calls twice. Night.

Far across the lake we can see the lights of Lake Hotel, the ranger station, marina, stores, cabins and trail-
erpark. On a good summer's night, Lake Campground
is one of Wyoming's more populous towns—thirty
thousand souls. Every now and then there's the pinpoint headlights of cars on a highway. At fifty-five miles
an hour the cars seem to be moving incredibly fast.

"It's as if we exist in two separate worlds," says Alisa.
"What can they possibly be seeing?"

· · ·

Awake to the sound of a motorboat. Watch it coming closer and closer as we make coffee in our long underwear, aware only too late that it's the white Boston Whaler of the law. Waves from twin Mercs crash ashore at our feet as the boat hovers broadside fifty yards off the beach. Too rocky for them to come in. We grin and wave into the telescope. A bullhorn rasps something about the fire . . . a violation . . . a citation. Communication is limited. We douse our meager flame and throw the hot rocks into the lake. Will this appease? Evidently, for the rangers roar off.

We gather our gear and pack the loads for the last time, scramble up to the trail, and begin hiking down along the lake shore to the highway.

New Year's at Canyon

FROM YELLOWSTONE LAKE'S OUTLET, THE RIVER FLOWS north into Hayden Valley, the sagebrush-covered remains of an ancient lake arm, named for the surveyor. Sixteen miles further and the river picks up speed, draws together, and makes a wild plunge over the 109-foot-high Upper Falls and then the 320-foot Lower Falls, roaring through mist into a yellow-walled canyon.

A highway joins the river at the lake's outlet, and thousands of tourists make the pilgrimage across Hayden Valley to the brink of the Lower Falls in their cars—next to Old Unfaithful Geyser it is the most popular part of the park.

Steven Fuller lives in a brown house on top of a hill at the northern end of Hayden Valley, a mile from the Yellowstone's falls. Fuller opted for a Peace Corps stint rather than a military tour in Vietnam and retreated into the African bush where he lived with Angela, an Englishwoman he'd met while a student at Leeds. Their first daughter Emma was born in Cambridge, Massachusetts, five years later. When Emma was two, he and Angie loaded their possessions into a VW bus and headed west to start a new life.

The bus broke down in West Yellowstone, Montana, in the valley of the Madison, western gateway to the park. It was November, and Fuller took the first job that came along—winterkeeper at Canyon Village, the tourist development on the north rim of Yellowstone's Grand Canyon. He knew only that the job entailed shoveling snow off roofs to keep them from caving in.

"It's the hardest job in Wyoming," said the grizzled old veteran whose place he was taking. He'd been winterkeeping for a quarter century; couldn't shovel all them flat roofs no more—and the Park Service only building more—waugh!—damn the Californicated architects.

But Fuller took to the hard work and isolation well enough, swimming in a sea of thought and slush among the rooftops and cornices, the pinetops and raven calls high above Yellowstone.

Summers he's a plumber ("the perfect occupation for a failed Taoist," he says) for the Yellowstone Park Company, a subsidiary of TransWorld Airlines, the park's chief concessionaire. Angela is Canyon Village's personnel director.

Fuller's goal is to explore all the places within sight of his porch: Yellowstone Canyon, Washburn Peak, the Mirror and Central plateaus, the Hayden and Pelican valleys, to know every lost drainage, every steam column and quiet cauldron within five hundred square miles.

He refers to the Hayden as "Mother." Each new day he sucks in the sulfuric scent of creation. Sometimes, when the moon is right, he says he hears the roll of the Precambrian sea. Buffalo graze in the yard. A grizzly once broke in a window and swiped a pot of stew from the stove. At night the roar of the Lower Falls booms in through an open window while pine martens settle their marital spats beneath the floor.

Nearly all of my journeys through the Hayden, those that haven't been made in a car, have been with Fuller in the winter, which is really the best time to see the park: campgrounds empty, no flutes or electric guitars, no hissing lantern light or Coleman stoves, no campfire smoke, no barking dogs or crying children, no television hum or glint of Airstream trailers, no autowinder camera bursts or Kleenex blowing, every building shuttered and boarded, hung with Closed for the Season signs. But for Fuller, the season's only begun.

I wake to slight noises in the kitchen and quit the down bag, dressing in darkness while Ree, the ferret, rustles around in her cage. Out the window, blue clouds turn pink above a landscape of snow and pine. Mist rises from the Yellowstone, and a gray winter fog steams out of a thousand vents and cracks, a vision so vast and fantastic and ethereal it can belong only to Yellowstone. Fuller, in long underwear and bare feet, lights the stove to boil water.

"Happy new year," he says. "Happy new year."

We take our coffee onto the front porch, scrape yesterday's wax off the skis—wood skis—and wipe pine tar onto the bases with rags. The bases are then heated with a butane torch until the wood pores enlarge and absorb the tar, staining them black. We can see our breath as we work. Next we rub a thick layer of paraffin onto the bases, melt it to a glaze with the torch, then stick the skis into the snow outside to cool while we collect lunch and load the packs.

Before moving to Canyon, Fuller had done a little mountaineering in West Yellowstone, but that was the extent of his knowledge. Experience has evolved technique, which is why he uses paraffin on his skis and not Swix or Jack Rabbit or one of a dozen other colored commercial varieties. "Snow is a variable," he says, "changing all the time. The Eskimo have twenty-eight words for snow. If I stopped to put on a different kind of wax for each different kind of snow, all I'd get done in a day'd be waxing." Paraffin seems to work the best over the broadest range of conditions. His skis were made by Laps and are much broader, longer, and heavier than their modern fiberglass counterparts. Fuller wears rubber-soled, leather-topped Maine hunting boots rather than low-cut leather shoes; a pair of green gaiters that extend to his thighs; a sheepskin cap of his own design that looks like something a Mongol might have worn; and large, oversize sheepskin mittens.

Yesterday the measurement of snow depth in the front yard was forty-eight inches, one-fourth of what will be there in March. Gone are the house's front steps; entrances and exits are made through a shoulder-high trench. A snowdrift reaches up to the roof on the house's backside.

"By the gauge, it's ten below," says Fuller as we clamp our boots into bindings.

We ski west, climbing gradually from meadowland into forest, powder snow shaking off pine boughs onto our shoulders as we slide around the trunks; drop into a small canyon with orange lichen walls and boulders pillowed beneath white. Water runs beneath the ice— the only sound. At the base of some willows I find a dead chickadee, three spots of brown fluid staining the snow next to its beak. Fuller shows me a cave where he and Emma spent the night once, and not far away we come across the remains of an elk carcass, red ribs and bits of scattered hair, the ground all around packed hard by coyotes.

Within an hour we've reached the summit of a ridge overlooking the Hayden, a hundred-square-mile desert of snow, wind polished as smooth as bone china, fringed by pine forests. To the east is the Yellowstone, its slow bends frozen, a few Canadian geese and goldeneye ducks concentrated in the open water amid chunks of ice.

Rather than giving us warmth, the sun's rise brings on a thick fog. I follow close behind Fuller.

"Wish some of this would clear," he says. "I'm having trouble finding a route."

At Alum Creek we pass the dark phantom shape of a buffalo, coat frosted, wagging its head down through snow to grass, too intent on survival to pay attention to us. The creek is warm enough to wade—one of Yellowstone's blessings—but waist deep. We carry skis, boots, and a wad of clothing to the other side, then dress and rewax the skis.

Jim Bridger claimed Alum Creek possessed powers of shrinkage, and stage drivers taking sports on the Grand Tour perpetuated the myth by telling of a woman who reduced her size eight feet to a size two.

We must make zigzag traverses to climb the first hill, planting the poles, kick-turning around, going a few more yards, and doing the same. As I rest, sweat drips onto my ski and freezes. Every thirty minutes we must rub on more wax and cork it smooth. Fuller worries that we haven't enough wax; if the snow cuts through the wax's protective layer and scratches the pine tar, the ski bases will begin icing. If the icing becomes bad enough we will have to walk out, floundering through waist-deep snow.

On the hilltop we find three buffalo skulls uncovered by the wind, snow spilling through the eye sockets like salt. Below us are a dozen buffalo, traveling single file, plowing a deep trough through the snow on their way to new grass. We can hear the slosh of fluid and the hollow rumbling in their stomachs as they move, whistles, sighs, grunts, and bellows. "They seem like ships passing," says Fuller.

Yellowstone's buffalo were originally mountain bison—*Bison bison athabascae*—smaller, darker, warier, and less gregarious than their plains brethren, direct descendants of the herds existing in the park after the last ice age. For a time after the park's creation it looked as if Yellowstone's bison might follow in the wake of the great annihilation taking place on the plains. Hunting in Yellowstone Park was not illegal—indeed, one of the attractions that drew early visitors was the fine hunting to be had.

From the first, the national park idea had been attacked as a waste of money and natural resources. Preservation did not fit well in harness with the industrial age. "I cannot understand the sentiment," stated one opponent, "which favors the retention of a few buffaloes to the development of mining interest amounting to millions of dollars."

Much of the public was indifferent, but sentiment was growing. As machines gave people more leisure time, that leisure was being spent out of doors, in the wilds. By the 1880s the Northern Pacific Railroad was within a hundred miles of Yellowstone, and tourists began visiting the park in droves. "The majority," according to one army lieutenant, "prowling about with shovel and axe, chopping and hacking and prying off great pieces of the most ornamental work they could find. Men and women alike joining in the barbarous pastime."

Private concessionaires served the visitors' needs and their own greed with bathhouses and chained bear cubs, pens of elk and buffalo, amusement rides, toll bridges, and firetrap hotels. On tour with his father, Ewing Sherman climbed Washburn Peak and penned,

"Society in general goes to the mountains not to fast but to feast and leaves their glaciers covered with chicken bones and eggshells."

"During the first five years the large game has been slaughtered here by professional hunters by thousands, and for their hides alone," wrote William Strong in *A Trip to the Yellowstone*, published in 1876, "but few years will elapse before every elk, mountain-sheep, and deer will have been killed, or driven from the mountains and valleys of the national park. . . . How is it that the Commissioner of the Park allows this unlawful killing?"

But the park's commissioner, Nathaniel Langford, was also its staff, and a full-time bank examiner for the territory as well. No funds had been allotted the new park, no authority delegated.

Five years after Strong posed his question, the park's second superintendent, Philetus W. Norris (whom Hayden described as a "gaudy frontiersman in buckskins and feathers") installed Mountain Harry Yount as the park's first ranger. But Harry resigned after the first winter. "I do not think that any one man appointed by the honorable secretary, and specifically designated as a gamekeeper," he wrote in his last report, "is what is needed or can prove effective for certain necessary purposes, but a small and reliable police force of men is what is really the most practicable way of seeing that the game is protected from wanton slaughter, the forests from careless use of fire, and the enforcement of all other laws, rules and regulations for the protection and improvement of the park." Five years later, the U.S. Army assumed command of Yellowstone.

The issue of wildlife preservation came to a head when the notorious buffalo poacher Ed Howell was caught red-handed in March 1894. A Captain Anderson tracked Howell to the mouth of Astringent Creek in the Pelican Valley, the Hayden's sister to the east, and, armed with only a pistol, crossed an open meadow in a snowstorm and got the drop on Howell as he skinned a buffalo. Howell's Sharps rifle lay within arm's reach, his dog was curled up asleep in the snow. Howell cursed and kicked at his hound swearing that he'd have killed Anderson if only that damned cur had warned him.

Emerson Hough was touring the park on assignment for *Forest & Stream* magazine at the time of Howell's capture and telegraphed the story to his editor, George Bird Grinnell. Grinnell fanned public outcry from ashes into flame. The next year the Lacy Act was passed, "to protect the birds and animals in Yellowstone National Park and to punish crimes in said park." Afterward, Howell often boasted that if Yellowstone had law and order it was because of him.

In an overzealous attempt to increase numbers of buffalo within the park, plains animals—*Bison bison bison*—from Charles Goodnight's captive Texas herd were introduced, creating a hybrid. The buffalo population now approaches a thousand animals, many of them residents of the Hayden. But there are no predators to check their growth; and though dead and dying buffalo constitute a large part of grizzly bear diet, especially in the spring, grizzlies only kill an occasional calf, and the herds, in their continual search for range, often move across the park's boundaries and have to be destroyed.

Fuller pushes off first, streaming down the hill onto the flats; then I, crouched in a tuck, skis chattering, snow sparkling around my knees like cold smoke. My cheeks sting and my eyes water uncontrollably, and just when I think my legs can't hold the position any longer, just as I begin to worry about the speed, I punch through the crust and somersault to a stop on my back. Fuller promised that I'd see stars on this trip, and I do.

Fuller is likewise sprawled. Falling doesn't bother him, but the destruction of symmetry does.

By noon the fog has burned off. We move across the Hayden's flats in a white heat, stripped to cotton turtlenecks, parkas tied around waists, faces greased with glacier cream to protect them from the sun. The snow has become soft and slick; we can glide eight feet at a stride, ski tips knocking snow from sagebrush tips. A few miles take us into a geyser basin that Fuller calls Grizzly Gulch. We take off the skis and walk on dry ground, carrying the gear. It sounds hollow underfoot—I place my feet exactly in Fuller's tracks, moving slowly among cavernous holes boiling with blue water, roaring cauldrons spitting mud. A steaming warm stream sheaths pine trees in frost and ice. Gnats hum about buffalo dung. Fuller says he found a bear track here on a warm day a month ago. His mustache is white from his breath. He thinks there's a den nearby.

"I'd like to see a grizzly in January," he says, and I, who would rather not, suggest that we move along.

I find a rock that Fuller says is vermilion, the sacred material with which Neanderthals painted their dead. A glint of obsidian catches Fuller's eye; he picks it up, holds it in his palm. It's been worked, a piece of arrow or spear point. "Probably a thousand years old," he says, tossing it off to the side.

Fuller says that at the time of the Pinedale glaciation, when Hayden Valley was a lake of melt, there were people here not much different in their physical makeup than us. He conjures a vision of hunting bands scrambling among the rotting pieces of ice around the lake shore. He believes the late Pleistocene was the original age of affluence, enough of everything for everyone. As resources dwindled with our increasing ability to exploit and waste them, government and laws evolved to deal with apportionment, creating, in effect, classes.

Placing our ears to a geyser's throat, we listen to it rumble far below and then come gargling up, waiting until the last possible moment before jumping back as it erupts, spewing us with a shower of warm spray. Afterwards on a nearby log we sit and eat lunch: half a grapefruit each ("colder than you can get it in Seville," Fuller says), toast, and sardines. Any remaining stomach space is filled with rolled oats.

Now and then we can hear the obnoxious whine of snowmobiles several miles away on the highway, like the buzzing of angry bees. "The technology exists to make them quiet, you know," Fuller says. "There should be a law against sound pollution in a place like Yellowstone. This is a cathedral, not an amusement park."

Though a National Park Bureau had been advocated in Congress as early as 1900, it was 1916 before the Park Service was actually created to "conserve the scenery and the natural and historic objects and the wildlife therein and to provide for the enjoyment of the same in such manner and by such means as will leave them unimpaired for the enjoyment of future generations."

Stephen Mather was the Park Service's first director, Horace Albright his able assistant. Mather's first task was to unify the twelve national parks then existing; each park was under separate administration and receiving separate congressional appropriations. To keep his darling Park Service alive Mather needed tremendous public support. Tourists. Roads.

Troopers had escorted the first cars out of Yellowstone Park; by the 1920s the Ford was welcomed with open arms. Hiram Martin Chittenden's efficient system of wagon roads was asphalted and made into the Grand Loop. In their wildest tourist hallucinations could Langford, or Hayden, or Mather have foreseen millions of tourists buying tickets to see their park? Seventy thousand of us a year loving it to death on the trails?

In 1887 the photographer F. Jay Haynes skied from Mammoth, park headquarters, to Canyon in order to make a winter photograph of the Lower Falls, which had never been done. The round-trip took him a month and nearly cost him his life.

As late as 1965 it took Tom McHugh, a photographer doing work for a Disney film, two days to snowplane into the Hayden Valley from West Yellowstone over snowcovered highways.

Snowmobiles started coming into the park during the late 1960s; even so, few penetrated as far as Canyon, and fewer ventured into the Hayden.

When the Fullers moved to Yellowstone in 1972, getting into or out of Canyon was still something of a winter adventure. After the roads closed in November, the nearest ranger was thirty miles away at Snake River Station. There was another winterkeeper at Yellowstone Lake. Until the snowplows opened the roads at the end of March, the Fullers rarely made it out or saw anyone else. Angie rode forty miles out by Snowcoach to the hospital when brown-eyed Skye was born. That was in 1974.

But a few years after the Fullers moved to Canyon, the Park Service began grooming the roads, making snowmobile trails, opening the way for hundreds of machines to reach the interior. Now the Hayden highway is busy year-round. Fuller says there is talk of keeping the Canyon Hotel open to accommodate cross-country skiers. Every spring the snowplows arrive at Canyon earlier—"it used to take a dozen men with snowshovels a month to clear the road over Dunraven Pass, now a rotary snowplow does the same job in a week." Rangers winter at Canyon and Lake stations, issuing tickets for drunken driving, investigating theft, fighting crime. Sometimes the Youth of America Conservation Corps shovels the walks around the Canyon's rims. There's a prefab warming hut in the middle of an intersection where candy bars are sold; and fifty yards away the filling station sells pre-mix. Fuller says a helicopter landed in the valley while he and Emma were having lunch on a hike one afternoon last summer; six smiling men with waving hands got out: a Geologic Survey crew checking benchmarks. "A gross and frightening misuse of technology." Here and there he's found tire tracks in the Hayden. Geothermal study people have been touching off blasts. One dawn last fall a helicopter came roaring up out of a meadow leaving behind a dead bull elk. "The best thing for Yellowstone," Fuller says, "would be to spare it the vandalism of improvement."

We leave Grizzly Gulch in fading light and blue shadows, skiing east toward the valley's center, cross Trout Creek with a sideways jump. This was once the site of an open dump used by the Canyon Hotel. As many as a hundred grizzlies picked through the garbage on any given day, and the trails of nearly three generations of bears came out of the woods as a wheel's spokes go toward the hub. The bears drew visitors, and, in time, the evening bear show became a major attraction.

A camera repairman in Jackson Hole once told me a story of inadvertently hiking into the midst of some bears bedded up a few miles from Trout Creek; he counted thirty-four grizzlies in the sagebrush surrounding him. That was while the Craigheads were doing their study, he said, and some of those bears were so close he could read the numbers on their ear tags.

John and Frank Craighead were trying to get a count on Yellowstone's grizzly population by identifying and tagging individuals; they estimated a population of about two hundred grizzlies, all of whom, at one time or another, utilized the dumps (there were eight scattered throughout the park) as a source of food. The brothers shot the bears with drugged darts, weighed them, estimated their age, took plaster casts of their paws—as individual as our fingerprints—put numbered tags in their ears, and tracked many others by radio collars.

Park Service biologists said there were twice as many grizzlies as the Craigheads estimated and there was a stable backcountry population that never visited the dumps. The dumps robbed grizzlies of their fear of humans, took away their instinct to forage naturally— thus closing the dumps would disperse the "garbage" bears into the wild and lessen the chance for human and grizzly encounters—even though only two people had been killed by grizzlies in Yellowstone during the past hundred years.

The Craigheads believed that closing the dumps would force the grizzlies not into the wild, but into the campgrounds. The dumps should be phased out gradually. The Park Service pushed for instant termination, and the ensuing debate brought an end to a decade of Craighead research.

The dump closures began in 1968. Between then and

1972, when Trout Creek was closed, thirty-five grizzlies were killed by rangers in campgrounds and fourteen people were mauled, one fatally. Grizzly hunting
was legal in all the states bordering the park, and bears
that did disperse often crossed the park's boundaries
and became trophies. Sheepherders killed others. Others were poached.

The Craigheads said that the grizzlies' birth rate was
declining, and, at the present rate of mortality, the bear
would be extinct within Yellowstone in another quarter
century. Park Service biologists said that after an initial
downward trend the grizzly population would stabi-
lize. No one knew, and no one knows.

In all his thousands of hours in the Hayden, Fuller's
seen only a few grizzlies.

I once skied across Yellowstone Lake to Park Point with
Superintendent John Townsley, a big man, fifty years
old, who laughed often, shaking the wool ball on the tip
of his long striped stocking cap. His father had been
one of Yosemite's pioneer rangers. Townsley had served
his apprenticeship as a Yosemite ranger.

The lake was bright and blinding white; ice settled
and rumbled under our skis. There were pressure
ridges and cracks, and pools of slush from the hot spots
and thermals beneath the lake's surface. Now and then
the lake would make a noise as if a gigantic bow had
twanged overhead, a hum starting at one end and passing to the other.

When we were out in the middle, seven miles from
shore, the superintendent told me that, several winters

before, three rangers had tried to cross the lake's south arm on skis. The last and lightest man broke through the ice. In trying to pull him out (they failed), the other two got wet. One passed out on the ice and froze to death. The other made it to the cabin, struck a match, threw it in the stove, and then blacked out. He only lost his feet.

Townsley had just returned from a speaking engagement in California. Everyone had wanted to know what was happening to Yellowstone's grizzlies. "I appreciate your interest in the grizzly," he told them, "wanting to give so much area to this and that. What I really think you folks should do is move everybody out of the Sierra foothills, remove all the agriculture from the valley, and then set aside twenty thousand acres and stock it with grizzlies. That's the best way you can save the grizzly." The room went silent.

"Everyone wants to tell us what to do with our grizzlies," Townsley said, "yet they're the same ones who've made their money out of selling that land and what not. It's not the working class that's interested. They don't have the time.

"More and more people are going to visit Yellowstone," Townsley said. "For every person hiking in the backcountry today there'll be a dozen in ten years. Do you put plastic outhouses in the Thorofare or do you have five thousand people crapping in the woods? Do you sit back and wait for a grizzly bear to drag somebody from their sleeping bag or do you close off areas of the park and let the grizzlies roam?

"A great many mistakes were made in Yellowstone.

It was the first, the great experiment. It'd never been tried. You and I may interpret 'for the benefit and enjoyment of the people' in completely different ways. We built roads, we fed the bears garbage, we introduced German brown trout and rainbows in the streams, we killed off the wolves that kept the elk herds in balance—elk were more appealing to the public. Now the elk girdle the aspen, overgraze the meadows, and starve to death by the hundreds every winter. We put out forest fires when we should have let them burn. It is still an experiment.

"Yellowstone will become whatever the public dictates. It is, after all, the nation's park. The Park Service merely holds it in trust. Ultimately the people will decide. We've still got time to prepare."

The Trout Creek road is still faintly visible, a wide swath beneath the snow. "Though the sky is pink," says Fuller, "and the white man's path is straight and fast, we should climb a hill for the sunset."

In alpenglow and shadow we sit visiting and waxing the skis—no hurry now—then drop off the crest into night. For a time I can see Fuller's vague shape in front of me, and then I cannot. "If you think it's dark now," he calls back, "wait until we're in the trees."

I watch the tips of my skis until even they are lost, then feel my way over Fuller's trail, gliding in his ruts. Often I stop to listen: the hiss of Fuller's skis up ahead, the booming of a geyser basin, miles away. Twice when I stop I think I hear movement. The air is much colder when we're traveling near creek beds; warmer in the meadows. Breezes travel between hills. I have no perception of depth. What I think are hills turn out to be flat. What I think is flat turns out to be a hill.

What's this? My ski tips stick out into space. Far below a flashlight blinks. "Steep," Fuller yells, then, "I've lost a ski." Something about a creek. "Ski's in it. No, no, it's not."

I take a deep breath, push off, drop into a tuck, fully committed to whatever's coming, feel the same rush of weightlessness that comes of falling, roaring down through the darkness, ski poles ticking off the snow behind. I make one turn. Another, bearing down, then feel the hill flatten. I straighten up and coast, chuckling to myself. Suddenly the bottom drops out from under me and I pitch forward, landing on my face next to Fuller.

"Buffalo divot," he says. "All right?"

"Minor lacerations," I say, feeling my lip start to swell.

He tells me of skiing down into a herd of buffalo one night. "Couldn't see them until Smith, the winterkeeper down at lake, and I were right on top of them. For a moment it was pretty scary because the buff took off, stampeded, and we were right in the middle, but after I saw that we weren't going to be trampled it was exhilarating. Quite."

On our way back we make a slight detour, ski down the highway a mile or two, turn off into dark timber, and coast down a narrow, twisting path. At the bottom,

Fuller releases his bindings, kicks out of his skis, and plants them in the snow. I do the same. Half wading, half stumbling, we make our way downhill, switch-backing through pines, until a pounding fills the air and the earth falls away. Yellowstone Canyon. Fuller walks to the brink—"watch the cornices"—I crawl on hands and knees.

"A problem with heights, ehhh?" says Fuller. "Never's bothered me."

At our feet, the Yellowstone plunges 308 feet down. The air pulses with its roar, and a rain of freezing mist pellets us with ice. By winter's end, Fuller tells me, a cone of ice built of freezing mist will reach nearly as high as the brink of the falls.

We stand in silence for a long time, staring into the void, watching water fall into the canyon and disappear into places no one will ever know.

To the east, the canyon walls seem luminescent, glowing a pale yellowish white in reflected starlight, rims cornice draped, columns of steam rising from cracks and holes.

"It is pretty, beautiful, picturesque, magnificent, grand, sublime, awful, terrible," wrote David E. Folsom, who with Charles Cook and William Peterson was one of the first white men to see it. A hundred and eleven years and millions of visitors later, the canyon still defies proper description.

Other canyons may be deeper or wider, though the Yellowstone's 1,200 foot depth and 4,000 foot width are considerable, but they do not have the falls, or the mountains, or the geysers, or the grizzly bears, or a wild river's soul. The Yellowstone. To stand here is to know the meaning of the name. In ten thousand years, nothing's changed.

Wearily, we climb back up to the rim and bind our boots back into the skis. We are in timber most of the way—too dark to see, but Fuller's skied this trail so many times he could do it blindfolded. Every now and then I call out and he flashes his light so that I can determine his position and travel toward it.

The last light I see is home.

Downriver

IN A CHILLING MIST, I CARRY THE RAFT DOWN A LONG
hill to the river's edge below the town of Gardiner,
Montana. Magpies squabble and flap among the junipers as I work and occasionally make teasing passes at
the dog. Curious ravens croak overhead, wings swishing. Cottonwood leaves have already browned and
blown away. When the clouds lift I expect to see snow
on the Absarokas. Soon, winter. The river looks cold,
unfamiliar, and fast.

It takes thirty minutes to pump up the raft, a gray
Campways Searider, fourteen feet long, seven feet
wide, a slightly pointed, upraised snout, and a rounded
stern—my home for the next five hundred miles. I secure the rowing frame to the raft with nylon straps run
through D-rings and clip nine-foot oars to pins star-
board and port. A cane canoe seat with a folding back
serves as a chair. Baggage goes in the stern, covered with
a green tarp, and lashed down with rope—many
strange hard lumps and bumps and points beneath canvas. Too much stuff for one, I think, but nothing goes
back up the hill.

Finished, I check off a list inside my head. All the boating paraphernalia's been packed. I've groceries, cartridges and dog food, wool mitts, hip boots, overcoat and scarf, and a new English hunting cap. Good-byes have been said. This morning I saw Alisa and Dean to school.

Rocking in a pool, the raft gives a savage tug at its leash. Time to go.

I coax Stryder, my hundred pound part collie part golden retriever, into the bow, take a last quick look around, a deep breath and shove off.

The current grabs the boat with more force than I'd anticipated and it takes one moment too long to scramble aboard. We're sucked left when we should be right, sent careening among rocks on the river's shallow side. A blast of ice water catches us broadside. The downstream oar stubs its blade on a rock, wrenches off the pin and out of my hand. While I'm struggling to shove the oar back on its pin, Stryder decides to abandon ship. Dropping the good oar I catch him by the collar, pin him to the floor with my feet.

By the time I've both oars in hand, we're washing sluggishly beneath the Gardiner Bridge, coasting the rollers out of town.

Somebody standing on the bank waves and points and yells, unheard above the Yellowstone's roar. I wave back and begin bailing water. Stryder shakes himself dry in my face, climbs forward, and sits looking downstream, nose in the air. And who cares what a landlubber might have to say anyway, ehhh? I warm up by rowing, ferrying back and forth, spinning to the left and right, getting reacquainted with moving water.

These first miles can be rough. In June, during flood, twenty thousand cubic feet of water a second snarl past the banks, water the color of creamed coffee boiling with debris—carrying whole trees and pieces, dead elk, broken bits of styrofoam coolers, outhouses, boards, and corral posts. Ten foot waves broad as a whale's back. A tenth that volume carries us now; exposed rocks hiss by like shark's fins, dark boulders lurk inches beneath the surface. The raft bottom occasionally scrapes gravel. Startled trout flee our shadow.

We're running west on a straight course between high dirt banks covered with sagebrush and autumn grass, jagged peaks of the Gallatin Range poking up to the south and west, steep Absaroka foothills east and north. Some houses' backsides up on the bank. Light flashing from the cars on U.S. 89.

Like water, civilization has followed the course of least resistance through the Yellowstone Valley. Animals first, migrating, wandering. Men following in their tracks. Then horsemen and wagons. The railroad. Towns. Blacktop roads.

Three plastic McKensie boats glide past willows on either side, somber guides at the oars, unsmiling clients casting from the bows.

On the Corwin Springs Bridge a red-haired kid in a yellow raincoat lofts a fish as long as his arm.

Corwin Springs was once known as Cinnabar, for Cinnabar Peak. For a decade Cinnabar was the end of the rail line for tourists en route to Yellowstone Park; from here they'd embark on the Grand Tour by stagecoach ("A strange vehicle," remarked one of Yellowstone's earliest tourists, the Earl of Dunraven, "mostly composed of leather. It was decorated with decayed leather; the sides were leather curtains; the top was leather; it was hung upon leather straps and thongs of the same material dangled from the roof."). Cinnabar Lodge boasted its own power plant, an irrigated golf course, hotspring bathhouse and a pine plank dance floor that accommodated a hundred couples. Calamity Jane hawked her autobiography *Beautiful White Devil of the Yellowstone* at the train station out front, and Specimen Smith stumped around selling "Specimens From Out of the Park."

"It is illegal to sell specimens from the park," an army officer told him. "Sign says 'From Out of the Park,'" quipped Specimen. When the railroad pushed upriver to Gardiner, making that town the park's north entrance, it put an end to Cinnabar's tourist dreams and the town died.

Sonny Brogan bought the lodge in the 1960s and turned the grounds into a pasture for his elk. In July Brogan cuts off the antlers of his bulls, sells the velvet to Koreans for forty dollars an ounce. The Koreans pass it on, either powdered or in round buttons as an aphrodisiac.

In the mid 1960s two freaked out characters murdered a hitchhiker near Cinnabar, cut out his heart during a thunderstorm as an offering to whatever demons possessed them, and threw the body into the Yellowstone. Two weeks later they were arrested in Haight Ashbury snacking on fingers. So mention cult and that, Charlie Manson, and Jim Jones are what people hereabouts think of; that's why they're wary of Ma Prophet's Church Universal and Triumphant buying the Malcolm Forbes ranch for $7 million and moving here from L.A.

At a press conference church members introduced themselves to the community, fifty ranchers standing in the Forbes tin barn, hats held in rough hands, white foreheads shining in the light cast from a television as students in a video ran around supermarket aisles dressed up like Uncle Sam shouting slogans. They'd come to Montana fleeing the holocaust towards which the rest of the nation was sliding, said Elizabeth Clare Prophet. Her people dreamed only of peace. The Great White Brotherhood's new home on the range, a golden Camelot by the river: a little Jesus, a little Buddha, a little Big Sur psychology—soul mates and twin flames, expanded consciousness, survivalism, astrology, mantra, and chants.

"It's nice to be here," said a member over the microphone, "you've got really great vibrations in this country."

For a time there was talk in Gardiner of forming a vigilante. The local preachers banded together, and the school principal banned church members' children. "Hell," said Brogan, "I might join." But in the end, like a lot of other valley residents, he sold.

· · ·

Up on Cedar Creek Bill Dexter sits in a lawn chair out front of his shack, watching the river, stroking that long gray beard like some old billy goat guru. Bill hauls his water out of the creek. Hasn't shaved in sixty years nor bathed in ten. Walks everywhere he goes, carries a Ruger Blackhawk forty-four—"en kin damn shore shoot 'er too." Keeps a year's supply of flour, coffee, and beans in fifty-gallon drums. Can't work hard or get around in the hills, can't run a trapline like he used to do. These days Bill spends a lot of his time just settin', meditatin', wonderin' perhaps why his woman left him for Hawaii so long ago.

Pretty Dick Randell started the state's first dude ranch—the OTO—on Cedar Creek in the 1900s, constructed a road going from here to there that crossed the creek thirteen times in two miles. Last spring vandals broke into the old cabin and sawed the antlers off all the stuffed elk heads in the den. Sold them, I suppose.

At the canyon's head I drop the oars in calm water and drift, check the load, tighten all the straps, zip and tie the life vest, kick off the hip boots, and lecture the dog about jumping out—"don't try that stunt here." In the next five miles the river drops four hundred feet. A gentle enough grade if you're walking it. But rivers move differently under gravity's influence than we. Given the slightest excuse, water boils and pours, backs up and around, falls over and through—an endless mixing of current within current, motion within motion. Given the proper volume and speed, water alone will create waves as it ricochets off bends and banks and piles onto itself. It is rocks that create rapids, that deter-

mine constriction, pace, and configuration. An incline
of twenty feet in a mile will give any water a voice; a
drop of fifty feet among rocks will make it roar. Ahead,
the dark lava rock walls of Dome Mountain part, re-
vealing the narrow-cut canyon of Yankee Jim.

The smell of deep water rises from down there, a
green smell, a fish and moss smell. An upriver breeze
blows cool against my face. An echo like a distant
storm. I nearly drowned in the river once. It was my
first river trip, first time in a canoe: Dick Greeves and I
with the mad gleam of St. Louis in our eyes. Dick had
said that a float trip would change my perspective, and
it certainly did. As our bow dropped over that first lip I
turned and asked what we should do, referring to bow-
pry, cross-draw, or j-stroke. I'd read all the books. "Best
technique," said Dick, "is going to be to try and save our
ass." Though we managed to do that, we lost some
other things, among them the reason for going on. That
was four years ago. Still, it's hard not to feel a forebod-
ing sense of déjà vu.

Oaring into the mainstream I concentrate on what's
ahead, the remembered route playing over and over,
like a mantra, in my head. A tree on top of a rock eight
feet above the surface, deposited during high water,
marks the point of no return.

Rowing hard upstream on the river's left side, feeling
the river's power trembling up through the blades into
my hands, I try to stay in the main flow until I'm fifty
yards above the first drop. Three-fourths of the river
funnels over a ledge and erupts into foam and a large,

erratic standing wave clapping backward over a hole that could hold a bus. Now I move left, hugging the shore, trying to stay off the rocks, straining at the oars. "Row! Row! Row!" I say aloud. There's no room for error. Banks blur as we drop down a smooth tongue into the first wave, bow-shattered crest drumming the raft like rain, wetting me to the chest, taking away my breath. Oars buck and jerk in my hands. We're lifted, then dropped, lifted again, and deposited in a long, calm, jade-colored pool. Turbulent boils percolate all around. Standing, I look downriver to the second drop, straining to see if there's anything I haven't seen before, didn't notice from the road, fighting back sudden doubts. Is there enough water to get through? What rocks are showing?

The river parts around a room-sized boulder, drops from sight. Foam flickers into the air like dragon's breath. Stryder stands with his front feet on the bow, nose pointed downstream, tail wagging. Rowing to the right, I line us up, then turn the raft sideways, raise the oars, and drift until we're hovering on the edge. Now I spin the bow first and tuck the oars in. The slot is so narrow I won't be able to use the oars until we're in the waves at the bottom. I lean forward, braced to drop the blades and pull as soon as we hit bottom. For an instant we hang on the lip, crashing whitewater filling the air, then fall in a sleek roller coaster rush over great hump-backed waves into the canyon's heart. Here the waves diminish, and we float silently on still water, all of the Yellowstone condensed by canyon walls into one turbulent pool thirty yards wide. A boil explodes from the surface, rears above my head, quivering like a block of Jell-O, collapses.

The canyon's named for Yankee Jim George, an ambitious, white haired, wild bearded Dutchman who anticipated making a living off tourists and miners and blasted a toll road across the rock on the mountain's south side in 1880. Five years later the Northern Pacific brought its line from Livingston to Cinnabar and put him out of business. Yankee Jim greeted each daily train with a shaking fist.

While staying at Cinnabar Lodge in 1903, Theodore Roosevelt sent a messenger downriver to summon Yankee Jim. He wanted to meet the cantankerous old cuss. Yankee Jim sent the messenger back with these words for the president: "You know where I live, Teddy."

Roosevelt was returning from Yellowstone Park where he'd had a bully good time showing off for his friend, the naturalist John Burroughs, rounding up elk badlands style. The president had amused the troopers at Norris Station by trying out their skis on April snowdrifts. He stopped long enough in Gardiner to dedicate the cornerstone of park engineer Hiram Chittenden's stone arch gateway. Roosevelt found it marvelous that "bits of the old wilderness scenery and the old wilderness life are to be kept unspoiled for the benefit of our children's children. . . . no nation facing the unhealthy softening and relaxation of fibre that tends to accompany civilization can afford to neglect anything that will develop hardihood, resolution, and the scorn of discomfort and danger."

From Cinnabar, Roosevelt sped west in his presidential car to Yosemite and a camping trip with John Muir. Muir was fighting desperately to keep Gifford Pinchot's dam out of his beloved Hetch Hetchy Valley and hoped "to do some forest good in freely talking around the campfire" with the president.

Drifting around a narrow bend we surprise five otters, all trying to cluster around a dead sucker on top of a midriver rock, too intent on running their hands over their slick catch to notice the boat. There's only room on the rock for four otters and the fish. The one left out swims around until he finds a niche, climbs on, and forces another off.

"Hello," I say, and they sit upright, wrinkling noses upthrust. All dive, dark shadows passing beneath the boat.

In the last set of waves a trout as long as my arm and as deep through the chest as the oar blade swims upriver just off the bow. Separated by a trough we rise and fall together three times and then he's gone.

Now the Yellowstone bends due north, a course it will maintain for the next fifty miles. A gentle, fast current, stretching out to feel its banks after the canyon's constriction, splitting into its first definite channels around small willow islands and gravel bars. To the south, Electric Peak in the Gallatins turns blue with distance. The peak was named by a member of the Hayden Survey whose hair stood on end as he approached the summit. A few years later John Muir advised the weak of spirit to climb it during their park visit and get a charge. The ruins of some twenty ancient redwood forests buried one atop the other in ash have been discovered near the peak, each forest maturing and flourishing and then being smothered by volcanic eruptions thousands of years apart. The unique thing is that some of the trees are still standing. . . . and there's petrified little birds in them singing petrified little songs just like Jim Bridger said. Yes!

The Absarokas are to the east, my right, dark peaks paralleling our course ten miles away, freshly whitened summits above lush stands of timber, like green velvet, seamed by ravines, avalanche chutes, and wild drainages. Mountain men called them the Yellowstone Range, appropriately enough. To the miners and early settlers they became the Snowies. Captain W. A. Jones, the first white man to cross them by what has become Sylvan Pass, tried to christen them the Sierra Shoshone. Finally, in 1879, they were officially named in honor of the Crow, whose name for themselves is Apsaruke. The old men say the word refers to a large bird no longer seen. In sign talk the people made a bird symbol with upraised palms touching heel to heel. French explorers mistranslated all of this into *"Gens de corbeaux"*— Crow. The Crow name for white men was *Beta-awk-a-wah-cha*, sits-on-the-water, because they first saw them in a canoe.

· · ·

We float past Mol Heron Creek, Slip 'n Slide, Joe Brown, and Tom Miner. It's almost dark by the time I pull us in to camp at an island at the mouth of Six Mile. Stryder plays with sticks while I unload. The sky is clearing, but out of habit I pitch the tent, build a fire, cook up some beans, and eat them with a warm tortilla.

My face is warm with sunburn, arm muscles ache.

The river turns to molten gold after sunset. A night wind sighs downriver, and house lights come on, twinkling like stars against the mountains. Honking geese fly past, low and fast, going upriver.

Up before dawn in pink light. Cold enough to form ice on the still pools at the edge of the river. Over a petty, sputtering fire I make coffee and cook breakfast, sit on a log scratching Stryder behind the ears, watching the sunrise over Emigrant Peak. A bald eagle skims upriver and coasts to a stop in a pine. Seven crows cross the river, cawing, wings flashing. Cattle bawl.

I scour the breakfast dishes with river sand, swirl rinse water as if panning gold, toss it into the current. Frost on dead leaves. Frost on the raft. I don gloves to shove off. Stryder, unsure about going with me this morning, waits on shore until the last moment, makes a leap, slips on the slick rubber, and takes a swim. Shafts of light break over the mountains through the cottonwoods turning water vapor into steam. Yellow cottonwood leaves drift alongside the boat, clinging to its sides.

· · ·

Jim Bridger wintered on Emigrant Creek with a band of Crow in 1844. "Thirty year have I been knocking about these mountains," I can almost hear him say, "from Missoura's head as far south as the starving Gila. I've trapped a heap, and many a hundred pack of beaver I've traded in my time, waugh! What has come of it, and whar's the dollars as ought to be in my possible? What's the ind of this I say? Is a man to be hunted by Injuns all his days? Many's the time I've said I'd strike for Taos and trap a squaw, for this child's getting old, and feels like wanting a woman's face about his lodge for the balance of his days; but when it comes to caching the old traps, I've the smallest kind of heart, I have. . . . but beaver's bound to rise, I say, and hayar's a coon knows whar to lay his hand on a dozen pack right handy, and then he'll take the Taos trail."

I have often wondered, and history doesn't tell if Jim spent his winter with one of the "coarse featured, sneaky looking, thick lipped, sharp nosed" young women, as described by an early trader, or one of the "hags who could be compared to nothing but witches or demons. Some of them of monstrous size, weighing 250 to 300 pounds, with naked breasts hanging halfway down to their knees. Barelegged, hair cut short and their faces smeared over with white clay . . ." Waugh!

Gold was discovered up Emigrant Gulch in 1863. Yellowstone City, as its three hundred residents christened it, became the first town in the entire seventy-thousand-square-mile basin. That first winter (the town lasted three) flour sold for a hundred dollars a sack, bacon a dollar a pound. Hanging was the penalty for murder, robbery, or insulting one of the town's fifteen women. There was supposed to be fifty million dollars in gold buried in the banks of Emigrant Gulch, but nothing much ever came of it, and nothing much is left: a few old buildings and sluiceboxes rotting up in the hills and ghost mines with names like King Solomon, Black Warrior, Morning Star, Bunker Hill, Iceberg, Shoo-Fly, and Avalanche.

Trailerhouses and condos are at the Emigrant's mouth now. The creek's dry, its mothering snowbanks used up, its water rained over hayfields all summer long. There are a half-dozen Land for Sale signs—another ranch's being subdivided to pay the inheritance tax, or being sold because the view's become a lot more golden than cattle. Some junked cars used for riprap have been pushed to the river's edge. The Church Universal and Triumphant owns most of this land. The small town of Emigrant will soon be called Glastenberry; Ma Prophet predicts a community of ten thousand.

In 1867 Nelson Story brought cattle in to feed the miners. The army detained him at Fort Kearney on the Bozeman Trail, telling him he couldn't go on without escort and they hadn't the manpower to provide him with one. But Story had brought something other than cattle from Texas—repeating rifles. He left the fort, and got through. The first crop of wheat was harvested in 1868. Though it sounds like a real estate developer's concoction, the early settlers called this place Paradise Valley.

During the Indian Wars, the residents periodically

fled paradise in flatboats and mackinaws constructed at John Tomislin's mill on Mill Creek. They were crude boats, roughly constructed, and in them the travelers suffered six weeks of blizzards and rocks and Wolf, Bear, and Buffalo rapids; were caught on sandbars and on snags; were bushwacked by outlaws, ambushed by Indians, and drowned.

"If it were not for the expectation of being fired into by savages every moment, the traveler would enjoy the trip hugely," wrote the fourteen-year-old son of Montana's territorial judge.

At Pine Creek the river takes the first downward tilt I've felt since leaving Yankee Jim. More channels, sharper bends, riffle dropping to pool, pool to riffle, a tapestry of mountains unwinding, golden cottonwoods and white Absarokas reflected in water. Mergansers patter downriver in front of the boat, Woody Woodpecker heads outstretched, wings flapping. I surprise two whitetailed deer drinking, and stop for lunch.

Taking my fishing rod I walk upriver to where the river pools at the base of white bluffs, an underground stream sweating down its face. Rings of feeding fish dimple the surface. I traverse the bluffs carefully, trying not to dislodge pebbles, tie on a wooly worm, and cast. The bug sinks just below the surface, and I strip it in slowly through a foam-covered eddy. Reel in, cheap reel clacking. Cast again, feeling the line straighten out and spring forward, straighten out again. The bug lands with a plop. A fish streaks for it, bumps it, and turns away. Another fish grabs it, turns, and I set the hook and bring a whitefish to bay. In ten minutes I've netted three more. Some people kill whitefish and throw them away—trash fish—but hungry and unprejudiced, I put mine on the stringer.

A fishing guide I know was once fishing this pool, caught a fourteen-inch whitefish, tossed it back, and was shocked to see a trout rise and suck it down.

Back on the river we pass all the regular things, cottonwoods and willows, mountains, ranchettes and cabins, prefabs here and there—first, second, third, and fourth homes—cows getting a drink. Past Deep Creek, Trail, Bullis, and Suce.

In the afternoon we pass through a narrow cut between Wineglass Peak and some cliffs to the east. The river's slowing down, pooling up before entering the town of Livingston. This place's name is Allenspur, a railroad siding, the proposed site for a three-hundred-foot-tall earthen-fill dam that would create a lake thirty miles long, inundating the entire stretch we've passed through today.

There have been plans to dam the river, of course, ever since the first farmer scorched a crop: for hydroelectricity; for flood control. Blueprints have come and gone. But nothing has seriously threatened the Yellowstone so much as coal.

How vast and valuable the Yellowstone's resources are. In 1832 it was beaver fur. In '68 it was gold. In '75, buffalo. In '82, the open range. A century later it's the river's misfortune to flow atop the largest strip-minable coal formation in the world.

Coal has always been a part of the Yellowstone's history. Early explorers mentioned black seams in the river's bank; fur traders and homesteaders used the coal for heat, railroads mined it for their engines. But interest remained low until 1970, when the Environmental Protection Agency decreed that the amount of sulfur particulate passed into the air through Eastern factory stacks must be reduced. Since coal in the West is low in sulfur and is more economical to obtain than Eastern coal, it was much cheaper for coal users to have Western coal shipped to them than it was to install the necessary stack scrubbers to remove the sulfur or to switch to alternative fuels, and it would be even cheaper to build power plants at the mine mouth and send the electricity direct.

No one in the Yellowstone Basin thought much about any of this until the publication in 1971 of a diminutive report entitled *The North Central Power Study*. The report predicted that by the year 2000, strip mines in the Yellowstone Basin would be providing coal to twenty-five mine-mouth power plants. Thousands of megawatts would hum toward Portland, Spokane, and Chicago. There would be coal gasification and petrochemical complexes, slurry pipelines, and a quarter-million increase in population. The whole of this development would be fed by the Yellowstone, mainstem and tributaries, either diverted into pipes or released as needed from dams. Allenspur was merely one of nineteen potential sites.

Two years later, draglines and power plant stacks were on horizons everywhere, and energy companies were talking about using the entire Tongue and Powder rivers. Nearly half of the Yellowstone's annual flow of eight million acre-feet was about to be tapped.

Though the Yellowstone is considered Montana's river by virtue of its main channel, it and its major tributaries, the Clark's Fork, Bighorn, Tongue, and Powder, all originate in Wyoming. Wyoming accounts for nearly half of river's seventy-thousand-square-mile basin. And while this basin is river rich, it's water poor. Rainfall averages less than fourteen inches a year. Whoever controls the water here controls the wealth, not to mention the destiny of fellow citizens and numerous mute life forms. Water is the basis of everyone's living—indeed, of everyone's life. Those who think themselves unaffected by it are only insulated. Peruse any basin newspaper and you'll find the Yellowstone mentioned somewhere in bold print. Too much water, or the lack of it, determines local temperament and economy. Ranchers and farmers suffering from drought buy few new pickups and do little shopping in town. If winter storms bring the elk down early, it fills native paunches as well as wallets. Even the man pulling your car out of a ditch with a wrecker says, "Yeah, that spring storm was a bummer but just think of what it did for the snowpack," not to mention his business.

And yet laws concerning water were so lax as to be virtually nonexistent before 1973. Until then you could still establish a water right on a stream or river by simply staking a claim and putting said water to a beneficial use. First in line, first in right. Use it or lose it. The predominant philosophy of water users is that water flowing downstream is water going to waste. Though it's technically illegal to do so, these water rights had been traded and sold back and forth for a hundred years. And industries establishing their rights on the lower Yellowstone said while it was true they were taking most of the water, they were using it for the most good.

In 1973 a panicked Montana legislature passed a Water Use Act that, among other things, placed a moratorium on industrial use of the Yellowstone's water until some studies were done and a public hearing held. The legislature wasn't as concerned with keeping the river from drying up as much as they were with trying to determine who owned how much of what.

Faced with losing their water supply, Montana cities and towns, irrigating districts, and government agencies all filed claims on a piece of the Yellowstone. Wyoming wanted to devote its share to energy. North Dakota demanded that the Missouri be kept full. The Crow said they owned development rights on the Bighorn by virtue of treaty. Two Yellowstones couldn't have provided enough water.

A public hearing lasted two months and produced five thousand pages of testimony, pro and con. Crusty third-generation ranchers said the country had all been wilderness and wild rivers once and not worth a damn until the white man came. Developers argued for development. Think of the jobs! The cash flow! An Iowa farmer wrote a letter wondering what was to happen to his corn. Jack Hemingway flew out from Sun Valley, Idaho, and said a few words on behalf of trout. All the networks flew in to watch, and for a time you could catch the story on TV.

Amidst all the uproar one man stood out, a white-haired spokesman for the Montana Department of Fish, Wildlife, and Parks, James A. Posewitz. Posewitz said that a river exists for itself. It's alive, it creates and nourishes life. By flowing downstream the Yellowstone was doing just as God intended. It wasn't going to waste. Posewitz spoke for the voiceless and voteless users, of the fluctuations in water levels and temperatures that triggered trout to spawn. Of the difference that a few inches make to a paddlefish trying to swim upriver. Lowering the Yellowstone would make goose nests more vulnerable to predators. A river has the right to the use of its own water.

Indecision prevailed until 1979, when Montana's Board of Natural Resources and Conservation granted the river a pleasant but tenuous victory in the form of a 5.5 million acre-foot instream reservation.

You don't hear much about the river's fate now, but the issue's only dormant. Our needs for water only increase. And out in the pine and gumbo hills draglines and derricks keep on gnawing into the earth, turning our history into fuel and fuel into our history, lighting our lights, turning us on.

Going down a side channel I come on a fisherman sitting on the bank eating lunch and drinking a can of Bulldog Ale.

"Hello," I say and he hello's me back. I hover in his eddy and visit.

"Catchin' anything?" he asks.

When I tell him I'm not fishing, he shrugs. He's about seventy, white haired beneath a red ball cap, and wearing a half dozen sweaters of various colors in various states of disrepair under a much stained fishing vest, black wool pants, and tennis shoes. He smells of willow and campfire and dank beaver pond and trout blood and liniment and old chew. He tells me he's fished every day of his life since retirement from the military. He used to run out from town when he was younger. Now he rides a bike. The largest trout he's ever caught weighed ten pounds.

He informs me that the pool I'm about to enter is named for the whorehouse that once flourished nearby ("Pity," he says, "pity"), makes me a gift of three trout (no catch and release man this), tells me to beware the experts, and juts his chin good-bye.

I drop down a small run to the head of a long calm where two fishermen work, their McKensie boat snugged to shore. One stands waist deep in the river, casting long, powerful casts to the channel's other side, letting his weighted streamer tap against the concrete riprap and slide down into the current. The friend watches, arms folded across chest-high waders, puffing on a pipe. I hold back on the oars waiting for acknowledgement. The man turns, wades further down, and begins casting again. I oar ahead.

"Damn you," he screams above the water's roar, "you're going over my fish!"

· · ·

The river has begun bending east, the Great Bend as it's called. It was somewhere along here that William Clark struck the Yellowstone in July 1805. Clark was descending the river to a Missouri rendezvous with Lewis. As they returned from the Pacific they'd separated on the Beaverhead and were exploring homeward by different routes, returning downriver without the prehistorics they'd expected to find but loaded down with wonders nevertheless.

Clark had eight men with him, the woman Sacajawea (wife of Charbonneau, mother of sixteen-month-old Baptiste), his black slave York, and eighty head of horses. He'd wanted to build canoes the moment they struck the Yellowstone but thought the current too rough for skin boats and none of the cottonwoods along the banks sufficiently large for dugouts. The party proceeded overland to the mouth of the Shields River, which they named for John Shields, a member of the group, and made camp.

Sixty-four years after Clark passed the Great Bend, Amos Benson established a trading post, saloon, and stage stop, and three years after that, tourists began passing through on their way to Yellowstone Park. Bill Lee built a wretched little ferry that they used at considerable risk.

In 1883 the Northern Pacific Railroad built a supply depot a few miles up from Benson's Landing, named it for a railroad trustee, surveyed it, platted it, and put it on the map: Livingston, Montana—elevation 4,900 feet. By the time the first Northern Pacific construction crew arrived, the town had five hundred citizens, two hotels, two restaurants, two watchmakers, two wholesale liquor dealers, two meat markets, two drug stores, six general mercantiles, a newspaper, and thirty saloons. Twenty thousand cattle and two hundred thousand sheep had summered in the vicinity, and the harvest had been thirty thousand bushels of grain and ten thousand bushels of potatoes. Calamity Jane was in town.

She'd been a scout for the army (disguised as a man) and said she'd been saved by a cold from dying with Custer at the Little Bighorn. She'd ridden for the Pony Express in the Dakotas, and would have killed Jack McCall when he murdered Wild Bill but in the excitement had left her guns at home. At the age of fifty she was described in the *Livingston Enterprise* as having "a deeply lined, scowling, sun-tanned face . . . with the leather-clad legs of a thirty-year-old cowpuncher." The reporter had found her at home smoking a cigar and doing dishes.

"I'm a rough woman, jedge," she told the court in her Ma Kettle voice when they awarded custody of her children to her husband, "but these kids allus have had a square deal from me. I ain't no saint, and yet I might be worse; I've nursed this man that's gettin' this divorce and I've saved his worthless life once; the law ain't givin' me a square deal—it never gives a woman a square deal no how."

Livingston itself sits like an island on the smooth buffalo plains, with serpentine Yellowstone curves shim-

mering up through the cottonwood leaves, blunt northern butt of the Absarokas, Mount Cowan, and Livingston Peak rising to the south, Crazy Mountains to the
northeast, Bridgers to the northwest.

Most of Main Street was destroyed by a fire in 1924
but here and there are two-story, false-fronted brick
buildings with painted advertisements for Coke-a-Cola
or Yellowstone Sport Cigars ("Every puff a pleasure")
on their sides. Though no one's used them in forty
years, there's still hitching rings in the concrete sidewalk outside the Mint Bar. The population's twelve
thousand now. There's three fewer bars than when the
train arrived.

We float past the lumberyard, a cement plant that's
been pouring its cement on the banks for years, an island covered by houses, a bridge with a canoe wrapped
around an abutment, past a golf course—duffers blasting balls—two bridges, a sewage pipe, and, finally, past
town.

Past Dry Creek, Billman, Fleshman, and Ferry.
Clear water, blue water, white water, green water and
all the tones in-between; riffles and deep pools, sand
and gravel beaches, slight bluffs and short grass hills
bright with unfinished construction, mountains turning vague with evening shadow.

Where Benson had his landing, we flush three geese
standing on a sandbar spit. In the deep whirling eddy
where the victims of Bill Lee's ferry drowned, a mallard drake squawks up. A fisherman lofts a big fish for
me to see.

Exploring a stray channel I see a pink-skinned

woman watching me from the bank. A tipi rises above the willowbrush, metal stovepipe sticking out the top. A man comes plunging out of the brush, jumps into the river off my bow, bounces up to the surface and runs onto the beach.

"We're having a good time," she says, "are you?"

"Yes," I say. Then I'm swept out of their life and into the mainstream.

A mile further and I make camp on a small island. Bake my fish with a potato and call it a night.

Wind this morning. Livingston is the second or third windiest place in the nation. People refer to thirty miles an hour as "breezy." Of course, it doesn't blow this way all the time. Sometimes, as the old-timers jibe, it blows ta' other direction, maybe a little harder.

By standing up I can see the props of wind turbines spinning, slowly, on Mission Flats. The potential is forty thousand kilowatts a year from one machine alone; there are plans for a hundred or more to be built within the coming years, a literal wind farm of energy. The day the first machine was dedicated there wasn't enough wind to turn the prop. A year later two machines were blown over. This must be one of those days.

We tend to think of wind power as a new idea but here and there along the Yellowstone are rusted turbines abandoned by ranchers and homesteaders after the coming of the rural electric association.

Past Mission Creek, Work, Locke, Peterson, and Hunters.

A new bridge is under construction at Springdale. I have to scoot beneath the work platform. Inches to spare, hand over handing it along the beams. A workman stops work and watches me pass. I lift my hand but he turns his back. Kids walking home from school across the old bridge stop to gawk and wave and menace me with stones.

Not long after that the wind drives me to the mainland. I can't row against it. Each stroke, with sore arms, is painful. Camp is in a wash among steers. Before dark I gather enough driftwood for a fire and start supper. Find a sandy spot to spread the poncho and sleeping bag, then sit watching the alpenglow on the Absarokas through cottonwood smoke, rubbing the soft spot on the dog's head with my fingers.

I'm caught half asleep in front of the coals when a storm blows in, tears a cottonwood limb from a tree and flings it down behind me. I put the tent up in a rainstorm, fall back to sleep listening to droplets pelt the nylon.

Awakening during the night to throw rocks at the cattle I find the rain has become snow.

October 13. Sitting huddled beneath a leaky tarp. Sixteen inches of snow on the ground. Still snowing. Parked on the beach the raft looks like a drift.

And how are things other than that? I forgot the axe and left my insulated boots on the porch; all the wood's wet. I'm out of kerosene, and the problem of condensation inside the tent is acute. The sleeping bag is wet.

I'm wearing all the clothes I brought and I'm still cold. Things like that. The annoyance of the moment is the accumulation of cottonwood smoke under the roof of my cook shack. Cottonwood seems to put out the least heat, burn up the fastest, and produce more smoke than any other variety of wood I know. When I can take the smoke no longer I go out and stand in the blizzard, a choice between eyes watering from smoke or eyes watering from wind and cold. Since the bark is soaked but the inner wood is dry, I spend most of my time peeling it. Dull work, but it passes time. I'd of built a better camp, but for the past two days I've thought this storm was going to break. Why build today when it might clear tomorrow, ehhh?

I'm only seven miles from Big Timber. Every now and then when the storm lets up I can see pinpoint headlights on the interstate.

My first discovery, yesterday, was that this was an island. It took thirty minutes to circumvent it. There's a large grove of cottonwoods in the center, tree branches filigreed in white, large flakes softly spiraling out of the sky. A horned owl lives in the woods, and deer tracks patter off on snowtrails through the rosebushes. I spent the afternoon rigging the tarp and gathering wood.

Today, feeling bolder, I wade the shallow channel at the island's back, climb up the bank, and walk to a schoolhouse. Small and white with a steeple, it looks like a church.

The teacher's name is Jane Grosvenor. "The kids call me Mac." She's taught here twenty-six years; she taught most of her students' parents and went to school with their grandparents. Her husband Frank is home with the cows. The school has one room, a potbellied stove, and twelve students in eight grades, shy, quiet, dryland kids in boots, Levi's, and skirts. Pictures of George Washington and Abraham Lincoln on the walls, cutout Halloween witches and black cats.

The kids ask me if I get lonely. Does the dog like it? Where does he sleep? Was I afraid? They tell me about the ranches they live on, their new puppies, and 4-H projects. You wouldn't get any of them out on that river. No way. No sir.

Jane's big fear is consolidation. The school board wants to close the one-room schools down. Not enough attendance. Not a good enough education. Bus the kids to town. "It's not true," says Jane, shaking her fist in the air, "look around! These kids help each other. I have time for every student. Our rural schools are the center of these communities. People vote here, have meetings, discuss issues, hold dances and parties. It's a crime," she says, "to close down these rural schools."

"I have to go," I say. "My fire won't keep."

Walking back I jump two mallards off the channel, drake and hen. As they flare and come back overhead I send both arcing into death with the shotgun—wings shredded, speckling the snow with blood, last of their body heat warming my hands.

By the time I reach camp my cheeks feel like ice and my overcoat tail is frozen stiff. I put wood on the fire, build it into a blaze, and sit rubbing my hands. When

the coffee's done I go out to sit on the bank in the snow
and skin the ducks, watching the feathers drift downriver, feeling an invisible sun drop, the temperature
going down. Geese returning from their day's feed yelp
overhead, beating their wings against the wind, going
upriver: flock after flock.

A meadowlark goes swirling by, wings fluttering,
beak gasping. It dips beneath a small riffle and doesn't
come back up.

I quarter the ducks and cook them on the grill over
coals, sweep snow off the tent fly with an oar blade, pull
all the stakes tight, unzip the door and ease myself in,
trying not to bump the sides; unzip the bag and crawl
inside. Stryder gets to sleep in the tent and tries to worm
his way in the bag by laying his head beside mine and
gradually working his way down. He makes it just past
the edge before the warmth knocks him out.

Snow falling from tree boughs collapses the tent and
sends me out into the dawn to dress. Chinook wind
blowing. Snow melting. Rays of sunlight shining
through broken cloud. River steaming.

Cold duckbreast for breakfast.

I bail melt out of the raft, load my soggy gear and
leave.

Dead leaves rattle across the snow on shore, eddying
among the rocks. Sunlight and storm squall. Frosted
Absaroka drift in and out of gray cloud. Ducks flush
from the lee side of islands and sloughs, pass overhead,
wings whistling, turn, and circle back to land in the

same places after we've passed. The wind's at my back,
generally helpful. Sometimes not, pushing me faster
than I want to go, into places I'd rather not be, but better that than blowing against me. I skid along where I
can, put my back into it and oar when I must. Stryder,
staying down out of the wind, shivers on the floor under my legs.

Around a bend the Crazy Mountains loom into storm-
light, bright, white, and severe. Named they say for the
crazy woman who lived in them. She'd been raped,
beaten, scalped, and left for dead. Through one bloody
eye she'd watched Sioux warriors play catch with her
baby's head and skin her husband alive. Liver-Eating
Johnson supposedly found her, built her a cabin, and
looked in on her now and then; he'd made a grim warn-
ing on her gateposts with some warrior's head.

The story doesn't say what became of her. Did she
gain her wits and go back East? Did she starve out or
just wander off?

When Robert Redford played Jeremiah Johnson in
a movie, he was playing a composite character based
loosely on the legend of Liver-Eating Johnson. Johnson, the story goes, married a beautiful Flathead prin-
cess named the Swan, left her pregnant while he went
away, and returned to find her and the child's bones
among the charred cabin logs. After that Johnson lived
only to kill Indians and avenge the Swan. He slit open
their bellies, grabbed out their livers, and ate them
before their dying eyes.

The real Liver-Eater bore little resemblance to Redford or the legend. Johnson weighed 250 pounds with a great shaggy head. He killed men with his bare hands, and had killed two soldiers at Fort Union by knocking their heads together. He'd gotten his name by eating only one Indian liver, though he'd shocked the disembarking passengers of a steamboat once by lining the gangplank with poles on which he'd stuck Indian heads. In his time he'd been a sailor, gold miner, soldier, scout, wolfer, woodhawk, and whiskey runner. Horn Miller, who had a reputation as a hard man in Montana Territory in those days, said the Liver-Eater was the toughest and meanest man he'd ever known.

In their later years both Johnson and Calamity occasionally hung out at Hunters Hot Springs on Hunters Creek. Dr. Hunter had been a surgeon in the Confederate Army who came to Virginia City to find gold. On the way he noticed the hot springs and later, when the gold didn't pan out, he filed for the land on the north side of the river and built a hotel. The Hunter family shot at raiding Sioux through loopholes in the wall of the house. Mrs. Hunter was the first white woman to live in Sweetgrass County; their daughter Emma was the first white child to be buried there. Their son drowned crossing the Yellowstone. The Crow liked the doctor, had saved his life once, but liked to raid his garden. They took a watermelon once but brought it back. "How should one prepare this kind of food?" the Crow asked. "It is not so good cooked."

After the railroad went through in the 1890s, the hot

springs made the Hunters rich. Their hotel boasted one
hundred rooms, the largest mineral hot bath in America, a bathhouse of 4,500 square feet, and "plunges," the
Livingston Enterprise reported, "large and small, vapors, tub baths, electric baths, vaporized for catarrahs
and acute bronchitis, sweating and rubbing rooms, a
natairorium with glass domes . . ." Clients came from
all over the world.

Nothing's left now. I pass a duck hunter crouched in his
blind. The river is clear and fast, flowing between willow and cottonwood banks, shattering into channels,
regathering often. Some channels are large, and we ride
them for fifteen minutes before rejoining the main;
some are creek size. Trout move ahead of the boat.

By noon we're blowing past Big Timber's grain ele-
vators and houses and a dump—a mound of rusted
cans, broken bottles, car bodies, pop machines, and
bedsprings pouring from the town's backside into the
river. Not far from the dump a warm spring trickles
down a small cliff: green grass and trees with yellow
leaves. A winter Eden. A one-legged man in a camou-
flage shirt fishes in the pool where the spring seeps into
the river. I row over to make conversation, eat lunch,
and share the storm, but the man reels his line in, turns,
places the rod in his teeth, and climbs up into the brush.
Retreating back to the middle I rest on the oars and
drift silently by, feeling his coyote eyes watching.

Past Little Timber Creek, Featherbed, Whitetail,
Big Timber, Boulder River, Otter Creek. The river's

getting greener and deeper and broader, less clear. Here
and there I find a ledge with a steep wave.

My friend Spike Van Cleve lived on Otter Creek.
Spike called himself pure quill Montanan. His great-
grandfather, Malcolm Clark, came into the country
with the American Fur Company in the 1840s. He
traded with the Blackfoot who called Malcolm Four
Bears. Calf Shirt once told Malcolm he hated all white
men but him least of all. But Malcolm died anyway, at
the hands of his wife's brother, Sword Tail, on the Little
Prickly Pear in 1869. Spike's grandfather moved west
with the railroad from Minnesota in 1887, bought
cheap cattle after the bust of the terrible winter before,
and took up a ranch north of Big Timber, which is
where the Van Cleves' westward movement halted.

Spike attended Harvard for three years but dropped
out to come home, marry Barbra, and whisk her off to
the head of Big Timber Creek and a rancher's life.
That was in 1934.

"A lot of men have degrees from Harvard," he'd say,
"but I'm the only one's got Barbra." They wintered on
thirteen dollars that first winter. "And would have lived
better," Spike said, "if I'd known as much about beans
then as I do now." At night they lay beneath wool blankets and elk hides, listening to the cabin logs pop with
cold. Next winter they had a child, Barby, and slept
with oranges to keep them thawed for juice. Every
night when Barbra lit the candle for the two o'clock
feeding, a lynx squalled.

Spike was sixty-eight when I met him ("The age," he
said, "when a man either can't pee or can't stop"), bow-

legged, pigeon-toed, full-bellied in the way ranchers get, wearing boots, Levi's, a grin, and a gray Stetson or a straw hat depending on the season. "Thirty years ago I could ride this country in the dark and know where I was," he often said. When I knew him he rode it, mostly, in a pickup. Not that he let that stop him from traveling familiar routes. More than once my head dented the top of Spike's cab as we bounced cross-country.

Once or twice a year he'd call me up and invite me over for a day of fishing. Though he thought my politics suspect—called me somewhat of an environmentalist—we got along well. I suspect he liked to have someone to open the gates.

One day I expressed surprise at seeing a wooden cattle guard. "The hell," Spike said, "I never saw a metal one till I was thirty years old."

Spike didn't like to fish the river. "Too big." His were plains streams, way out, with hardly a clump of brush lining their banks, damn little water, and extremely wary trout. "Mind, watch for rattlesnakes now."

He fished as if he were playing chess, setting up his moves carefully in advance. He stalked pools, pinching a fly between his thumb and forefinger, snapping it over a hummock into the water from a crouch. My technique appalled him. I lost so many flies that he took to carrying a dozen Joe-Hoppers just to loan me after I'd gone through all my own. He never seemed to mind, just grinned. As we fished or drove, I listened to Spike reminisce.

In every shadow and cleft and creek and coulee Spike

had a memory of something, someplace, or somebody. A story. Cole Pruitt kept his prize stud horse in the house so the Indians wouldn't steal him. Mrs. Franklin's running water was a trapdoor in the cabin floor. Here was where Sim Roberts killed Nate Young in '99. The horse thief Charlie Brown escaped from the Melville jail, took the sheriff's steed, and left a thank you note. The Englishman Mr. Jack loved a fast horse and kept two wives. When he was busted for moonshining, neither the city nor the county jailers would take Dirty Jim McQuinlan, and none of the barbershops would clean him up, so the agents had to let him go. The Norwegian homesteader with the last name Ohmeo who named his two sons Ome and Omy. And that's just a few.

When the Yellowstone was threatened by Allenspur Dam, there was a movement to protect it under the Wild and Scenic Rivers Act. The united front of the Van Cleve family helped kill the bill. Spike said there was too much land being locked up in wilderness, put under government control. Grizzlies have no place in the modern world, just like the buffalo. He wouldn't mind hearing a few less coyotes. Don't even mention wolves, he saw enough of those as a kid. He cursed because he had to get a permit from the Army Corps of Engineers just to replace the washed-out bridge across the creek. "I love the United States," he said, "and I wouldn't live anywhere else, but I sure am tired of the United States telling me how to run my business. The only outfit that can tell me what to do is my wife."

I went to see him while he was in the hospital in Livingston. He had a blood clot in his leg. The doctors wanted to cut the leg off. "They can go to hell," he told me. "What could Ol' Spike do with one leg?"

We talked for an hour. It was arctic outside and I'd just come from feeding cattle with a friend, bundled up in wool. Spike said the toughest thing about winter was trying to get a half inch of prick through four inches of wool, and we both had a good laugh. And then the doctors came in frowning, and I had to go.

I saw him a month later in Bozeman. I'd just come out of the hardware store and there he and Barbra stood. Spike had on a bright new scarf and his Stetson, one boot, and a shoe. He had to wear the shoe because of his leg. He said he felt a whole by-God lot better than when I saw him last. "My hired hand's been arrested and sent to the pen for cattle rustling," he said. "Hell, a good attorney'll get him off on insanity. Man'd have to be crazy to steal cattle these days at the prices they're bringing." We talked about the weather and the economy. He said people now days took too much for granted, took for granted things that should only be luxuries. People hadn't had running water in his day. Now they expected it, just like they expected cars and electric lights. It was too cold out to catch up on everything. Barbra was waiting. We both had things to do. We shook hands. "You come fishing with me this summer," he said. "We don't live that far apart." Halfway up the block he turned around and yelled something at me, waved, grinned, and then limped across the street.

That was the last time. Three days later he sat up in bed, watched the sunrise touch the Crazies, and died.

Past Cox, Dry and Milligan creeks, Upper and Lower Deer, Sweetgrass, Spring, and Hangman.

The wind picks up in the afternoon and rowing becomes so painful I begin hunting a camp—something sheltered and out of the wind and deep snow. I find nothing until I'm a mile past Grey Cliff Creek and it's almost dark, then there's an island on the left-hand channel facing sandstone bluffs. A hundred frightened geese take off from the island's point, bleating into the wind, voices echoing off the cliffs. I'm too tired to struggle with the tent, so I string the tarp between cottonwoods for a windbreak, clear away the snow as best I can, and build a fire with tinder taken from a cedar tree up close to the trunk. Curse again about leaving the axe.

Supper over, I put all the wood on the fire. While it pops I study maps and dry my overcoat and gloves. Stryder sits with cocked ears looking off into the dark.

Clark saw his first pelican on this stretch of the river; deer and elk were scarce. They'd passed an Indian fort built in a circle out of logs, about fifty feet in diameter and five feet high. "The squaw informs me that when the war parties (of Minnit. Crows, who fight Shoshones) find themselves pursued they make those forts to defend themselves."

The squaw Clark refers to is Sacajawea, the Bird Woman, a Shoshone who'd been captured by the Minataris and brought to live among the Mandans by her half-breed husband Charbonneau.

"Long ago he had developed a distaste for his own race," wrote Bernard De Voto describing Charbonneau at age seventy-five. "He was an Indian now, a good one, and lived with his people, not at the fort. He was as bent as a scrub cedar on a bluff, his face was as seamed as a claybank, but he was more sagacious than his overlords . . . and could travel river or prairie, forever, winter or summer . . . all the West and all its Indians, three generations of chiefs and traders, had engrossed on his mind an incomparable pageant." And the old man was still gambling for women and fathering children for a decade after that.

When the fire becomes embers, I go to bed, watch stars, and listen to geese pass. Once I wake to the sound of rain and pull a poncho up over my head.

Before light I wake, dress, take the gun, and stalk along the shore over sand and gravel through the willows to where the geese sleep, dreaming in the quiet water. Mist rises from the river. The fallen leaves are wet and silent. A lone goose raises its head, blinks, honks, folds its beak back beneath a wing. I think of where they have been, of all they have seen. Stryder whines. Every goose's head is up at once, like hundreds of periscopes, bright black eyes on me. A ripple of surprise goes through them, then alarm. A murmur of wings like wind. An explosion. A lifting goose, neck outstretched, white half moon cheek against the dawn, stutters, misses a wingbeat, falls. This is wrong I think as I pick up the goose, but I'm not sorry, wolfing down slabs of roasted goosemeat in front of the fire an hour later.

The day is bright, the river fast. At the oars, basking in the warmth, I feel I could spread wings and fly. Instead I tuck the oar handles beneath my knees, fill my pipe, pour a cup of coffee out of the thermos, review the maps like the morning paper and ponder what day of the week it's become.

Past Bridger Creek, Work, and Hump.

At the end of a channel I find myself at the end of a fisherman's line. A retired railroader and the railroader's wife, both wearing striped engineer's caps, are sitting on upside-down milk cans, bobbers bobbing on the surface of a deep pool.

"Doin' any good?" asks she.

"Not fishin'," me.

"Doin' any good?" she asks again.

Unclamping a cigar from his teeth, the old man spins around on his can, hollers to her face, "Can't you see, woman? He ain't fishin', he's travelin'!"

Travelin'. Yes. Drifting along backwards watching the Crazies turn blue with distance. Stretched out on the stern, Stryder makes dog sighs of contentment. If I watch the bottom rocks, it looks like I'm going fast. In reality maybe three or four miles an hour.

On the beach outside the town of Reedpoint an Indian girl guarded by three vicious malamutes shampoos her hair. As I drift by, Stryder and the brutes exchange growls.

"How many people live here?" I ask.

"Ninety-seven," she says.

Suddenly there's the wail of an ambulance siren.

"Make that ninety-six," she says, smiling. "Don't you get bored?"

Bored?

Do I look bored floating along picking stickers off my wool pants? I listen to all the water sounds, read the channels, trying to figure out which are faster, which are dead ends. I watch clouds, guess at the weather, take clothes off or put them on, look for the telltale heads and wing flutter of ducks, a deer's back or ear in the gray willows. Kingfishers dart around on shore, magpies black-and-white flit in the cottonwoods, a slow heron flaps. I've counted seven bald eagles today. Sometimes snow geese pass overhead, squeaking, white bodies like a constellation of swirling stars. I talk to the dog, row the boat, think. It's interesting to me. But instead of telling her that, or even saying no, I float on past, silent, leaving the question uncaught to fall and float like a stick to the Missouri. Bored?

Past Whitebeaver Creek, Whistle, and Section House.

The cottonwood yellows are not as bright, but there are more leaves on the trees than there have been. The beaches are gravel, bleached white. The wind has died, nothing but the river moving, broader, greener, deeper now. Splitting into channels, sometimes as many as a dozen. Lots of drowned cottonwoods with the river roaring through their roots. Snags. The bank gets undercut and they topple in, beavers bring them down. Spring flood leaves them stranded on the beaches, stripped of boughs and bark, polished smooth, colored gray, lying alone or in twos and threes, cracks and crevices packed tight with half a century's flotsam. Bits of willow from the Thorofare perhaps, pine cones from the Absaroka.

Channels veer off and carry me further away from the main river. Islands and trees get bigger, which must have pleased Clark. To protect the horses' hooves from prickly pear, they'd made them shoes out of green buffalo hide. One of the hunters "rammed a stob into the muskeler part of his body" near here. Rather than wait for the wound to heal before moving on, the men were so anxious to get home they built a litter and mounted it behind a horse travois-style. There was another good reason for haste: Charbonneau had seen smoke coming from a bluff a few miles away. Indian sign.

At sunset I make an island camp in the twilight shadow of gray cliffs. A cold breeze pours past me on its way downriver.

Lots of beaver sign: stumps with fresh shavings piled around, beaver-chewn trees lying on the ground, a network of beaver paths through grass and willow. While I'm eating supper, a beaver makes an upstream V close to shore, catches my scent, slaps the water with his tail, and dives from sight.

All night long I wake to the sound of him checking the boat out, getting scared.

A still, frosty morning. Sunday. I take my time getting dressed. A clean shirt, and for the first time since the blizzard camp, just Levi's, no wool. Moccasins in place of hip boots. Basking in the sun with my coffee I watch Stryder gnaw on a bone. Then I leisurely pack and shove off.

Pine-covered hills on my right, to the south; wind sighs through pines on the crests, pines run down ravines to the river's edge. Lush cottonwood forests spread to the north. A shingled barn roof goes past now and then. Five mule deer watch me from a beach, ears wagging. A bald eagle sits in treetop, and another circles in the distance.

As the day burns on there are geese in wavering lines and high V's overhead. A white bird that I think is a snow goose turns out to be a pelican.

Outside the town of Columbus, not far from where the Stillwater River joins the Yellowstone, I moor the boat and scramble up the bank for a visit.

Only the New Atlas Bar is open. It's dark inside. The walls covered with stuffed animals, some whole and some in part—numerous bull elk and bighorn rams, white-tailed bucks with strange racks, an albino fawn, a trio of mountain goats, a two-headed calf, a bobcat with a clock in his middle—old faded photographs of the town in its prime, and yellowing newspaper clippings of the same era. Old men with hard-times American Legion faces sit chuckling and mumbling and silent over their beers and Bloody Marys at the wooden counter. There are two of everything in the mirror. Brass spittoons on the floor. Fans turn slowly overhead. Farmers play cards at three tables in the back. A room off to the side is decorated in red velvet with private booths and buzzers. Conversation stops when I enter.

"What'll it be?" asks the bartender, polishing glasses. He's a slight, aproned, silver-haired gentleman in a worn panama, with garters around the sleeves of his white shirt.

"Just passing through." Me.

"Duck hunter?"

"Floatin' down the river."

"I'll tell you what," says the bartender, "more men have been killed over water in this country than over women."

Pulling past the Columbus Bridge I nod to a pair of fishermen baiting their hooks. With a sweet sense of relief I row on. The river's picking up speed, gathering itself tighter. Waves, where there are waves, have a sense of power about them, rolling beneath the boat like muscles.

When most of the river veers toward open country, I take a sliver going south, a stream barely wide enough for the raft. To squeeze beneath an undercut rock, I swing the oars in, resting the blades on the bow. Beyond the rock we twist down a roaring chute, skid through shallows, oar blades scraping gravel on either side. Twice I have to get out and walk, sloshing along in my hip boots, leading the raft by the bowline until the channel's deep enough for it to float.

Brown sandstone walls several hundred feet high on the right bank, pocked with thousands of holes utilized by nesting swallows. Geese flush ahead of the boat and wheel against the cliffs, beating themselves into long floating lines. Deer tracks in the sand. Cottonwood boughs stretch over the channel, the outermost leaves almost touching the cliffs, forming a golden canopy. Shafts of sunlight fall onto the water. The river steams where it's touched by sun. Steam and shadow, shadow and steam. Droplets from my oar blades ripple still pools in arcs as I row. An eagle sitting on a tree limb ruffles himself in the sunlight, shuffles his yellow feet, cocks his head, excretes a white stream halfway across the river, gives me the eye.

In a pool I cast for trout with a spinner, letting it slap against rocks and topple down, water clear enough that I can follow it, sinking, for several feet. A few minutes later I've two medium-sized rainbow trout—frying pan size.

Resisting the temptation to nap, I opt for a swim, one dive that brings me quickly to surface and back ashore to stand in the sun and dry in the wind while two redtail hawks circle overhead.

Past Keyser Creek, Brown, Hensley, Tutt, Tucker, Allen, Cow, Tilden, Cole, Valley and Bellion.

"I deturmined to have two canoes made out of the largest of those trees," wrote Clark in his journal at a location somewhere in this vicinity, "and lash them together which will cause them to be Sturdy and fully sufficient to take my small party & Self with what little baggage we have down the river. Had handles put in the 3 axes and after Sharpening them with a file fell[ed] the two trees which i intended for the canoes, those trees appeared tolerably Sound and will make canoes of 28 feet in length and about 16 or 18 inches deep and from 16 to 24 inches wide."

As some men worked on the dugouts, others prepared hides or hunted. During the past two days the party had killed seven deer, eight elk, an antelope, and two buffalo. But the Crow had taken half the horses (so much for the smoke). Three men were sent overland to the Mandan villages driving the remainder. Clark and his party, proceeding downriver by boat, would meet the horse herd at the Bighorn's mouth to assist them in fording.

I spend most of the day beneath the bluffs and cliffs, in the Yellowstone's backlands, until the threads and rivulets and channels all join and I've no choice but to be carried away. The north bank becomes blank and flat where the bottomland has been cleared for farming. I pass barnyards and rooftops, horses and sheep. Two waterfalls tumble into the river from pipes on top of bluffs. A few miles further and the Clark's Fork River comes in on the right, muddy from the recent snow, brown water mingling with the green, all of it becoming dull. On an island just down from its mouth I make camp.

"The beaver country begins here," wrote Clark. He'd mistaken the Clark's Fork for the Bighorn and wasted time waiting for Sergeant Pryor to bring the horses. But poor Pryor was having problems, alas, for the horses were Indian trained and took off after every buffalo herd they passed.

Jack Crandall, Horn Miller, and six other miners struck gold at the head of the Clark's Fork in 1870, but Indians killed two of them and stuck their heads on pick handles, with a coffee cup placed in front of each. So the boys moved on to other prospects for the winter. They and dozens of others returned in the spring to stake their claims on the George Washington and Republic mines, the Elkhorn and Miller Mountain, the Daisy and Homestake, becoming the founding fathers of Cooke City and the New World Mining District. A three-hundred-pound waitress named Little Eva served the miners their food in the restaurant, and the gravedigger Loco Brown buried them. Though the mountains were rich, there wasn't any economical way of getting the ore to market, and Cooke City never reaped the benefit. In Cooke City's gone to hell seclusion Ernest Hemingway wrote the first draft of *Death in the Afternoon* and the last draft of *To Have and Have Not*.

In 1877 the Nez Percé Chief, Joseph, led seven hundred of his people and two thousand horses down the Clark's Fork to the Yellowstone. They were leaving their beloved Wallawalla homeland, fleeing the threat of an Idaho reservation. Joseph hoped to cross the Canadian border and join Sitting Bull. They'd been hounded by the army of General Howard all the way and had thrashed the troops at Whitebird Canyon and the Big Hole. In Yellowstone Park, Nez Percé warriors killed two tourists, left another, Jessie Cowan, for dead, and made a miner named John Shively guide them through the Absarokas. Some hot-blooded young warriors supposedly destroyed Cooke City's smelter, taking lead (or silver) to cast bullets. Horn Miller climbed a peak for a look-see at the Indians and made the biggest gold strike of his life.

In gaining the Clark's Fork, Joseph had tricked a commander named Sturgis into thinking the Nez Percé had gone up the Shoshone; but once he got turned around, Sturgis pursued with a vengeance. He stripped his force to fifty men and two howitzers and made a desperate attempt to catch the Nez Percé at the Yellowstone. His mission was to delay them until Howard arrived with the main force. Howard had lost a son in the Custer fight the year before and most certainly wanted an opportunity for revenge.

Sturgis caught Joseph at Canyon Creek a few miles downriver—he'd seen smoke from the stage station they'd fired—but found his prey too hot to hold. Four bluecoats were killed and eleven wounded before Joseph and his people slipped away behind a dust cloud.

Civilization greets us with sirens, helicopters, car horns, beacons, towers, and dark dirty water. It's Billings, Montana, population 57,000, largest city in the basin. Down past the KOA campground (nation's first) and the power plant (Reddy Kil-o-watt blinking a neon hello), I drop the oars and drift beneath Sacrifice Cliff.

The Crow called this the Place of Skulls. You hear a number of stories, and varying reasons, but here some Crow warriors blindfolded their horses and rode off the cliff singing their death songs. Some say it was a grieving war party that returned from a raid to find their village decimated by smallpox. Others say it was done to drive the disease away.

In June of 1875 the steamer *Josephine* docked here, at the highest point anyone had brought, or would ever bring, a steamer up the Yellowstone. Her captain, Grant Marsh, carved her name and the date in a cottonwood trunk.

Grant Marsh had run away from Pittsburgh in 1845 to work as a cabin boy on the Allegheny. He was a roustabout on the Ohio, the Mississippi, and the lower Missouri; then a mate carrying the wounded from Shiloh Church to St. Louis in 1862 on the *John J. Roe*, "a boat so slow," Mark Twain wrote, "that when she sank it took the owners five years to discover it."

Marsh took his first steamer up the Missouri to Fort Benton in 1867, carrying miners to the Montana goldfields. Such was the flurry of activity—all those Civil War veterans trying to make a new start—that steamers were docked for a half mile above and below the landing. Other pilots discharged their cargo and went south; Marsh kept his boat at Fort Benton until autumn and took the miners back to St. Louis to spend their earnings. In doing so he risked getting iced in or stranded by low water, but as luck would have it, he succeeded, gaining a fortune for himself and the boat's owners and establishing a reputation for daring that attracted the attention of the army and the lucrative government contract.

The next year Marsh ran the steamer *Nile* up the Missouri in October to deliver annuities to the Indians at the mouth of the Grand River. He was frozen in before he got there and spent the winter against the east bank of the Missouri. A prodigious walker, Marsh spent the time exploring the surrounding country, making frequent trips to and from Fort Thompson, an Indian agency twenty miles cross-country. In preparation for the winter he'd unloaded most of the boat's cargo on Cul-de-Sac Island forty-seven miles downstream and inspected it almost weekly, making the round-trip in two days. The denizens of Fort Thompson, no doubt fighting winter boredom, pitted their best walkers against Marsh in races and failed; poor losers, they served Marsh a meal of stewed dog disguised as venison and then imported a Sioux known as Fast Walker to beat him.

Fast Walker didn't walk, he trotted, and vanished from Marsh's sight after only a few miles, made it to the island, ran twenty miles further, rolled up in a blanket for a few hours, and then trotted another seventy miles to visit relatives camped upriver.

In 1873 the army wanted to explore the Yellowstone for places to establish forts and picked Marsh for the job. No steamer had ever gone up the Yellowstone; its current was thought too fast, its channels too narrow. Yet Marsh took the *Key West* to the Powder River's mouth 260 miles upstream, in five days. A New Yorker turned westerner named Yellowstone Kelly shot game for the crew with a rifle he'd named Old Sweetness.

On his return, Marsh was asked by the army to run the *Key West* back upriver, to serve as a supply boat for a troop of cavalry escorting and protecting Northern Pacific Railroad surveyors. The cavalry's commander was none other than George Armstrong Custer. The regimental band played concerts under the summer moon for *Key West*'s crew. Between bouts of fighting Sioux, Custer and two English friends coursed wolves and jackrabbits with their hounds.

General Alfred E. Terry, the commander in chief of the western army, made a little speech to the officers aboard the *Key West*, saying that "this was the most interesting of all the Indian campaigns. What with English Lords, scientists and outsiders of every military description you would imagine it a big picnic."

Two springs later, Phil Sheridan, the new commander in chief of the western army, contracted Marsh to take the *Josephine* upriver to the mouths of the Tongue and Bighorn rivers just in case the army should ever need to establish posts or move troops into the vicinity. For protection against hostile Sioux, the *Josephine* carried a hundred soldiers and a Gatling gun with ten thousand rounds of ammunition. General James W. Forsyth—the hero of Beecher's Island in Colorado—was the army commander on board. Four scouts, among them Lonesome Charly Reynolds, ranged ahead and to the sides looking for hostiles. Marsh fully expected to be fired on around every bend, from every bluff, but the only Sioux they encountered

fled without firing a shot. In a feat of steamer navigation that was never duplicated, Marsh brought the *Josephine* past the Bighorn to this point, turned around,
and sped back to the Missouri in a record four days.

During the winter of 1876–77, P. W. McAdow
started a trading post near where the *Josephine* had
moored. A half dozen years later the place's name was
Coulson—home of Chicago Jane's Boudoir. There
were sixteen graves in Boot Hill, a brewery, a sawmill,
five saloons, a post office, and thirty other assorted
buildings, but no jail. Liver-Eating Johnson was the
sheriff for a time; he never used a gun, preferring to
"whop" the unruly with his huge fists until they saw the
light of justice. When the railroad pushed a few miles
upriver and platted out another town, Coulson's residents abandoned their town and moved as well. By October of 1882 Billings had 2,000 people, 155 businesses,
99 residences, 6 railroad buildings, a church, and 25
tents. Because it grew so rapidly the town was nicknamed Magic City. Now Boot Hill overlooks refineries,
and Josephine is the name of a disco.

Dark forces me to a beach next to the railroad tracks a
few miles from town, exhausted, depressed, the
stench of city in my lungs and clothes. Seven white-
tailed deer flush out of my campsite, a sandy wash
among three trees. I gather firewood from the largest
log jam yet. Soon after supper, rain drives me into the
tent.

· · ·

I make a mistake this morning in lingering over pancakes and have to pack the boat in a storm. As soon as
we're on the water, the wind begins, strong and cold,
forcing me into a poncho. To move at all I must row
with my back downstream, looking over my shoulder
to see where we're going. Rain pelts the water like
buckshot. The wind creates waves a foot high. Stryder
curls up on the floor. Ahhhh for the life of a dog—just
let ol' massa take care of things.

Over the sound of the wind and water and flapping
poncho I listen for the telltale roar of Huntley Dam, the
second largest diversion on the Yellowstone. The dam
waters an irrigation project, in season allowing pumps
to suck up 4500 gallons of water a second. The dam is
poorly marked and has killed ten people—high school
kids and fishermen who get drunk or daring and think
it can be run.

There's a channel going around the dam on the left
that appears to go all the way through, but I get out, tie
the boat, and go for a look anyway. The dam extends
across the river's main channel, dropping water over an
eight-foot-high ledge, transforming it into foam; a tree
caught out in the middle rolls over and over in the current.

The channel around the dam is passable and sheltered, but when I leave it the wind shoves me across the
river and pins me against shore. I must wade, pulling
the boat by the bowline, until I've got water deep
enough to get purchase with the oars. Then I heave
back out into the current.

Another mile and I stop at the town of Huntley, born

of the irrigation dreams behind the dam, snug the boat to a piece of concrete riprap, and walk in on main street. At the general store I buy a sweet roll and hang out by the wood stove, my trench coat dripping onto the wooden floor.

"Lord," says the counter matron, "what would a body be doin' out on that river today?" I have no answer.

At the filling station I ask an eighty-year-old jack of all mechanics if he's any kerosene for my lantern. He shakes his head no.

"Number-one heatin' oil'll do the same," he says and takes me around back to a 1936 tank truck from which he pumps a quart jar of the same. When I ask what I owe, he says, "No charge to a fool."

In the Red Dog saloon I have a shot of whiskey to warm up with and another for luck. Cheers to a fat, red-cheeked beet farmer and the barmaid, both watching TV. The newscaster's talking about drought. Barges are already unable to navigate the Mississippi sandbars. Each day a million gallons of water seep out of the New York City sewers. Some restaurants are using disposable plates so they won't have to wash and serving water only if it's requested. "In fifty years," says the newsman, "the Great Plains will be a dustbowl." He's conserving by taking only two showers a day.

"Anyone heard the weather?" I ask.

"You're going to get stormed on," says the barmaid and the farmer's hard "Hoo hoo hraw" laughter chases me out the door into the rain.

Past the Huntley Bridge I hug the dirt bluffs on the left, but am forced, in seeking deep enough water, to get back out into the main. By midafternoon the rain has become snow, blowing so hard that the river's a blur. My arms hurt from rowing, each pull sending pain through my shoulders, hands growing numb from holding on to the oar handles so tightly. The moment I let up we're blown toward shore or blown back upriver. Every hour I stop and walk to warm my feet. Hundreds of ducks in the air, passing me like bullets. More ducks flush from each point, twisting and circling overhead, landing again after I've passed. The temptation to shoot costs me eight shells.

I find a camping place in a secluded wooded spot on the left bank. Only eight miles since dawn. Willows and young cottonwoods are as thick as porcupine quills; dense stands of cane and yellow marsh grass, and green reeds higher than my head. To find a decent place to sleep that's not marsh or thorn thicket or stone, I must walk several hundred yards inland. Since I expect to be here several nights, I carry most of the gear up from the raft: the kitchen box, camera gear, clothing bag, shotgun, books, dog food, tent, sleeping bag, and water jugs. While carrying the cooler across a slough, I'm startled by a pheasant flying up under my feet, trip over a beaver-chewed log, ages old, and fall into a muddy hole—spilling the cooler and all its contents into the water. Lying there, feeling the wind and snow pounding my back, I want to give up and fade away, to dissolve and awaken in some other place. But I pick myself up, take off my gloves and overcoat, and begin groping around in the water until my hands are too cold to feel anything.

The tent is wet before I get it pitched, and the rain fly is torn out of my hands twice by the wind. I've misplaced the tent stakes and must use sticks to anchor the corners. Somehow even the sleeping bag's soaked. While I boil oatmeal, droplets of water sizzle on the fire ring.

Taking a walk, trying to settle down and think, I find that this isn't the mainland but an island. Its interior, beneath the cottonwoods, is a jungle of rosebushes; its edges are all willow. I wander up one sandy wash after another until it's dark and I'm lost. Stryder takes off after something and doesn't return when I call. The deer trails are too dim to follow and everything looks the same. Stumbling and cursing through the willows and rosebushes, I walk cross-country until I hit a beach, follow it, knowing eventually I'll find the boat, nearly falling over it when I do.

Across the river are the lights of Huntley, and not far away the glow of Billings. It must be all of six, I think. People over there are in snug houses, watching the news, sitting down to supper. I could row across the river, cache the equipment, and hike to town. Go home. That's exactly what I'll do tomorrow, I promise myself. Enough of this.

Back at camp the fire's dead. A wind torn bough has crushed the tent. The sleeping bag, though wet, is passably comfortable, and I draw up beneath a willow, drape ponchos all around, and sit zipped up with my back against the tree.

"Happy birthday," I say aloud. "Happy birthday."

An inch of snow on the ground this morning, melting fast. Sinister gray clouds dispersing, pink bottomed with dawn. A meadowlark singing.

I tarry long after the sun is up, drying things, hanging clothes on the brush. Everything steams, even the dog, passed out on his side in a patch of yellow light. "And how was your night?" I ask him. "Deer-chasing, pheasant-flushing, worthless hound."

It takes all morning to pack the boat, my promise of the night before forgotten amid the warming optimism of sunshine and blue sky. What, me quit? The river is fast and smooth and clear, spilling quietly around snags and islands, shattering into more channels than ever before, winding past sandstone bluffs that have been eroded into strange shapes, half domes and mushrooms, crumbling turrets and spires. Chunks of sandstone as big as the raft have fallen into the river. Ponderosa pines and junipers on the left bank, cottonwood bottoms stretching for a mile or more on the right. I spend the day drifting, spinning in lazy circles, stripped to long underwear top and Levi's, smoking my pipe, turning an oar only when I have to go bow first through a wave or miss a tree, enter an interesting channel, or investigate something on shore. Occasionally a puff of wind carries the sound of a beet harvester, the faraway grind of a truck changing gears on the high-

way. The Russian olives on one island are full of blackbirds, the bushes on another full of wrens. A prairie
falcon darts overhead. Swallows zip around among the
bluffs. Three bald eagles circle above. Ducks and geese
jump into the air every few hundred yards. A weasel
pops in and out of holes and cracks in the rocks on
shore, following me. A raccoon with a shiny bit of shell
in his paws looks at me, sniffs, and shambles off like a
small bear.

Past Pryor Creek, Twelvemile, Crooked, Razor,
Cabin, and Rock.

At Baptiste Creek I tie up and go ashore to visit Pom-
pey's Pillar, "a remarkable rock situated in an extensive
bottom on the Stard Side of the river and 250 paces
from it," as described by Clark. "I ascended and from
its top had a most extensive view in every direction.
This rock which i shall call Pompy's Tower is 200 feet
high and 400 paces in secumpherance and only accessible on one Side which is from the N.E. the other parts
of it being a perpendicular cliff of lightish colured
gritty rock on the top. There is a tolerable soil of about
5 or 6 feet thick covered with short grass. The Indians
have ingraved on the face of this rock the figures of animals and near which I marked my name and the day
of the month and year . . ."

The pillar's present owners have made it a park.
"PRIVATE PROPERTY. CLOSED FOR THE SEASON. NO TRES-
PASSING. VIOLATORS WILL BE PROSECUTED." The under-
growth's been cleared for picnickers; there's antique
wagons, petrified wood from seven different states, the
ruins of a wooden dugout ("DESTROYED BY VANDALS")

the Jaycees paddled downriver in honor of Clark, and a log information booth painted red and white with a wooden silhouette of Lewis and Clark on the roof.

The trail up the rock's side is wide and packed hard. There are railings ("DO NOT LEAVE TRAIL") and benches. Halfway up there's strange hieroglyphics, some left by Indians and some by visitors. Grant Marsh chiseled his name in the rock on the way to Billings. Some of Custer's men were here. (Before or after, I wonder, they were caught bathing in the river by the Sioux?)

Clark's imprint—Wm Clark July 24 1806—is protected beneath bullet-proof glass in a wooden frame that's padlocked and bolted into the rock. Bronze plaques honoring Clark (donated by the Masons) surround his signature.

Looking south from the summit, past corn stubble and the highway, I can see the faint blue shadow of the Beartooth Mountains, the crest of the Bighorns two hundred miles away. To the north are piney prairie hills and beyond them the plains. East and west the river shines in braided channels little changed since Clark stood here.

I'm tempted to stay on the pillar and see what spirits might walk on a full moon October night, what magic may linger, but a beet truck rumbles across a nearby bridge and I flee to the boat as startled as a deer.

Clark named the pillar for Sacajawea's son Baptiste, born in the expedition's first winter camp with the Mandans in 1804. Clark had nicknamed the boy Pomp, had worried about, tickled, and played with him for the better part of two years. Was he in love with Pomp's mother by the time they arrived here? Sacajawea was sixteen when she joined the expedition. Clark had ministered her labor pains and saved her life once. She called him Redhair, was eighteen and worldly now, had obtained horses for the expedition from her people, been across the mountains to the Big Water, seen a dead whale, and mistaken seals for the underwater people of her legends. Her laughter was the only music in camp. True, she was Charbonneau's wife, but he had three.

No one knows for certain what became of her. John Luttig, the Missouri trader, recorded that one of Charbonneau's wives died in 1811 and had been buried in South Dakota; which one he didn't say. Twenty years after the expedition, Clark compiled a list of surviving members and wrote "dead" beside her name. Did he do it with a tear? And yet on the Wind River Reservation in Wyoming a Shoshone woman, who many think was Sacajawea, died in 1884, at the age of one hundred. The woman, according to interviewers, had an intimate knowledge of the expedition; Sacajawea's name is on the tombstone up among the Indian graves. *Quien sabe?*

Clark went on to become Indian agent for the Louisiana territories, a speculator in furs, the governor of Missouri. He'd promised Sacajawea and Charbonneau that he'd take Baptiste and put him through school when he came of age, which he did, but the boy proved too wild to civilize.

· · ·

A quarter mile below the pillar, I camp on top of a smooth mainland bank. Beans and tortillas for supper. I look across at the sunset glow on the bluffs and watch sparks from the fire trace up into the sky. A big orange moon rises full above the cottonwoods; a flock of geese passes across its face, voices crying like flutes.

Frost on the dog this morning. He doesn't move from his curl until long after I'm up. Usually it's he who does the waking. Water's frozen in the water jugs. Ice in the still water at the river's edges. A hundred geese roar off a point as I shove the boat off.

Sunshine fades into clouds, and the wind comes up cold, hinting of snow. Not again, I think, humping up at the oars, but the wind only takes the clouds away. I spend another warm day adrift on a slow current, meandering the hours away beneath piney bluffs, avoiding snags, exploring narrow channels, contemplating all the hoo-doo sandstone shapes. I'm still drying gear out from the storm: socks, shirts, tent, and sleeping bag spread out on the raft's tubes.

Ducks flush around every bend; flight after flight of mergansers wing their way upriver. There're more snags than ever before, whole trees blocking channels, hoary old rips with pointed branches just breaking the surface. Carp roll in the shallows.

Sometimes I make a misjudgment and have to wade the boat through a tight spot, walking it along, pushing or pulling, whichever works.

We float until the sky is sunset pink, stop on a back

133

channel tucked beneath sandstone cliffs, jumping two
buck deer as I beach the raft. I follow a beaver trail
through the willows back into a cottonwood glade,
gather dead wood, build a fire, and wait for the moon-
rise.

When it's light enough, I pull the boat out into the
channel, clamber aboard, and sit in the still water at the
oars thinking about what I'm going to do. Two owls
hoot. Geese settle into sleep on a sandbar. I drop the
oars, pull, and feel the boat slip into the current. It's
much faster and blacker than I imagined, and for a moment I panic and try to grab the eddy water and scoot
back to shore, but it's too late and we're sucked out into
the night. I lift the oars and listen, straining to see, to
divine, to feel what's ahead. Is that a snag or an island
or a gravel bar or a rock? Is that the roar of rapids or a
dam or merely faster water? A flooded creek could
have washed new boulders out into the current, a bluff
could have caved in, a tree could have fallen. This is
foolishness, I tell myself, you'll be lucky to stay dry.

For the first time in many days I zip the life jacket
and kick the hip boots off. Even Stryder's tense, alert on
the stern, standing on all fours, ears cocked, lifting his
nose to taste passing scents. I try to stay in the main
channel, in the middle, gauging how far off the banks I
am by how deep I can drop the oars. Echoes. Water
sounds. I follow the quietest path. Sometimes we drop
down a channel so fast a breeze brushes my face. In
pools I drift, listening: water laps at the boat, beaver
slap their tails, ducks squawk and flutter, geese pass,

frightened mergansers patter, fish feed, from the brush
come chitters and squeaks and rustlings. A cow bawls.
A pickup bounces down a road.

At the Bighorn River's mouth I park on a sandbar
and watch green water flow into green water in white
moonlight. Water from Dunoir Creek, muddied by our
packhorses last August. Water from Deadman Creek,
Big Bull Elk, War Man, Rotten Grass, Two Leggin,
White Man Runs Him, Owl, the Little Horn, Sunday,
Slaughter, Sorrel Horse, and Tullock, to name a few.

There are eagle pits in these bluffs, places where
medicine was made, prayers said. Laughter in the river
bottoms. Feasts. Women gossiped among the rosebushes, bathed in these pools. Lovers curled beneath
buffalo robes in the moonglow. Absaroka.

As much as it could be possessed by any this river
country was possessed by the Crow, beautiful people of
the high prairie whose painted lodges drifted in the
wake of the buffalo. In the seventeenth century they'd
quit the Hidatsa in an argument over a piece of tripe
and left the Missouri and farming life to roam the Yellowstone, becoming its nomads, fighters, lovers, and
thieves. The Crow possessed some ten thousand horses,
three animals for each man, woman, and child. Cheyenne, Blackfoot, and Sioux were enemies. With the Hidatsa and Mandan, the Crow bartered horses, mules,
and clothing for the guns, ammunition, axes, kettles,
and awls of European traders. With the Shoshone
(when not at war—Washakie once cut the heart out of
a Crow chief in a duel on top of a butte), the Crow

traded axes, kettles, and awls for Spanish bits and blankets. Crow men were superstitious (nearly every aspect of their life was ruled by dreams), fierce in combat, prized their long hair (the locks of a noted chief measured ninety-nine hands in length), gambled for horses and wives. On ordinary occasions a man painted his face red and wore a tinge of yellow on his eyelids. The women produced the most beautiful beadwork on the plains, but cut off so many fingers in mourning for dead relations that an unmutilated hand was a rarity. Crow women could strike camp and be on the move in half an hour.

"On these occasions," wrote Robert Denig, a trader among the Crow for twenty-three years, "both men and women dress in their finest clothes. Their numerous horses are decked out with highly ornamented saddles and bridles of their own making, scarlet collars and housing with feathers on their horses' heads and tails. The warriors wear their richly garnished shirts, fringed with human hair and ermine, leggins of the same, and headdresses of various kinds, strange, gay and costly. All kinds of bright colored blankets, loaded with beads worked curiously and elegantly across them, with scarlet leggins, form the principal portion of the dresses of the young men or those whose feats at war have not yet entitled them to the distinguished privilege of wearing hair. . . . The women have scarlet or blue dresses, others white cotillions made of dressed skins of the bighorn sheep, which are covered across the breast and back with rows of elk teeth and sea shells. These frocks are fringed along the edge and around the bottom. The fringes are wrought with porcupine quills and feathers of many colors. When traveling, the women carry to the horn of the saddle the warrior's medicine bag and shield. His sword, if he has one, is tied along the side and hangs down. The man takes charge of his gun and accouterments in readiness for an attack however sudden. The baggage is all placed on the horses, at which they are very expert. Kettles, pots, pans, etc., each have their sack with cords attached. These are on the sides of the animal, and on top of the saddle is either one large child fit to guide the horse, or two or three smaller children so enveloped and so well tied as to be in no danger of falling. Often the heads of the children are seen popping up alongside of pup dogs or cub bears on the same horses . . . The great number and good quality of their horses make a showy appearance. Both men and women are capital riders. The young men take this occasion to show off their persons and horsemanship to the women. A good deal in the way of courting is also done while traveling. The train is several miles in length, wives are separated from the husbands, daughters some distance from their mothers, which opportunities are not lost by these young and enterprising courtiers. They ride up alongside, make love, false promises, in short use any and all means to obtain their end. . . ."

"The Crow country is good country," said Chief Arapooish. "The Great Spirit has put it exactly in the right place, while you are in it you fare well, whenever you go out of it, whichever way you travel, you fare worse. . . ."

And, of course, the Crow country was so fine the white man wanted it for himself:

Trickle of white became a flood,
keelboat sail,
smoke, belch, steamer breath,
wagon tops,
whohaws and goddamns,
Christian Sharps turning the buffalo to bone,
white like snow all around,
smothering,
covering.

Only a century and a half elapsed between the coming of the horse and the coming of the engine.

The Crow signed a treaty at Fort Laramie in 1851—the white man needed to build a road, and a road, after all, was only the width of a wagon. The Crow signed a treaty again in 1868, giving up all but the lower Yellowstone Valley. When gold was discovered on the Clark's Fork, a treaty in 1878 took away the mountains. When right of way for the railroad was needed in 1880, a fourth treaty left the Crow 2.5 million acres along the Little Bighorn. Pretty Bull signed it, his mark. Wolf Bow, Mountain Tail, White Horse, Poor Elk, Shot-in-the-Jaw, White Forehead, Pounded Meat, Bird in the Neck, The Swan, Blackfoot. Their marks.

"You say the railroad is coming up the Yellowstone,"

Blackfoot spoke, "that it is like the whirlwind, and cannot be turned back. I do not think it will come. The Sioux are on the way, and you are afraid of them; they will turn the whirlwind back."

The Crow signed their last treaty, if you want to call it that, in 1981, when a federal court awarded custody of their sacred Bighorn River to the state of Montana. None of the makers of states, the treaty signers, or the writers of compacts had foreseen the time when water in the West would become more valuable than beaver, cattle, or gold.

The Crow Reservation sits atop the new western standard of wealth, coal. The issue split the tribe into sides—traditionalists versus developers. An old story in the West. At a minimum level there would be three strip mines on the Crow Reservation producing 90 million annual tons of coal; there would be three gasification and liquification plants that would need 186,000 cubic feet a second of Bighorn water to run. From this the tribe would net $36 million in annual annuities—cash, not blankets and plows and food. But what the Crow really wanted was the chance to determine their own future. They demonstrated on Two Leggins Bridge, wept into the television cameras nationwide, and went to Washington, D.C., to plead their case with the Great White Father. It did no good. Police attended the demonstrations with dogs and riot guns, politicians made their usual futile gestures and promises, and the television cameras went on to other news.

Last August I rented a yellow Ford Pinto in Billings and drove south to attend the Crow Fair, the annual cel-

ebration the Crow hold near their agency, at the heart
of their reservation on the Little Bighorn River a few
miles from where Custer made his last stand on the hill.
I took the old road, not the interstate, and stopped at
Pryor to pay my respects to Plenty Coups and drink
from his spring.

When he was ten years old, Plenty Coups climbed
into the Crazy Mountains on a vision quest. He climbed
to the mountaintops and fasted, called for helpers. He
saw grizzly bears in the moonlight, but none of them
spoke to him. He cut off a finger and beat it against a
log until the blood spurted toward the sunrise. He
passed out. Four war eagles watched over him while he
dreamed. The spirits took him deep into the ground.
He walked naked through a narrow passage among
buffalo. Their wool scratched him. It was hot with their
body heat.

He was afraid of being crushed, of being killed by
their horns, but nothing happened. The buffalo were
going up onto the earth through a hole. Plenty Coups
saw that they covered the plains. And then they were
gone. Other animals emerged from the hole and took
their place, animals like buffalo but with spotted hides
and long horns. He saw a great forest. The Four Winds
created a storm that destroyed all but one tree. He saw
an old man in strange clothes sitting by a spring.

"Plenty Coups," the wise man said, "you have had a
great dream. You have seen the white man's cattle take
the buffalo's place. We have seen these animals with the
spotted hides about the traders' forts. The forest you
saw was the tribes of the plains, the storm, the white

man who will destroy all who resist. The one tree left standing is the Crow. The Crow must befriend the white man or they too will be destroyed. The old man is you Plenty Coups, in white man's clothes. You will be a great chief. You will change and lead our people on a new path, into a new age. You will help us be that one tree left standing."

It was sunset by the time I reached the pink and blue and yellow government houses of the agency. At the dancegrounds I took my place in a long line of cars proceeding slowly through the camp. Hundreds of tipis lined the roads, a few painted, most made of shining white canvas, strips of bark dangling from fresh-cut lodgepoles, smoke rising from fires—people eating and visiting and cooking outside beneath cottonwood arbors. Old grandmothers shuffled across the road in high moccasins, looking neither right nor left, intent only on where they were going, heads covered by shawls, calico dresses bound at the waist by thick leather belts. Young men in Levi's carried stereos blaring the Talking Heads. Packs of children rode horses bareback. Dancers were getting dressed, walking in clusters here and there. The air was rich with the sound of sleigh bells and drumming and horses nickering. Dust hung in yellow shafts among the cottonwoods. Some of the people had been camped here for a week, more were arriving. Everywhere I looked, a new tipi was rising, a new tent was being pitched, a new arbor was being raised.

The dancing was scheduled to begin at 8:00 P.M. but

did not actually begin until 10:00—Indian time. The dancegrounds were encircled by a ring of concession stands selling cotton candy, buffalo burgers, Navajo tacos, fry-bread, lemonade, ribbon shirts, and jewelry, hand-painted signs garish in the blinking Christmas tree lights. From game arcades powered by portable generators came the whizz, bang, and pop of Pac-Man and Zaxxon. Small boys paid quarters for a chance at the skill-crank. Broken water spigots spewed continuously, creating mud holes here and there. Already the trash bins were overflowing.

At its conception in 1903, the fair was intended as a place for the newly domesticated Crow to show off their prize potatoes and quilts. But the Crow turned it into a tribal gathering, a fair celebrating the things they held important—who among them had the fastest horse, was the best dancer, the best singer, the fanciest dresser, the most skillful rider.

Four groups of musicians were situated around the dance circle, the Teton Ramblers, Nighthawk Singers, Mad Dog Singers, and Singing Elk. Each clustered around a drum, taking a turn at warming up. Four badly wired speakers crackled with the announcer's voice in Crow. Close to grand entry time, the grandstands, seven tiers high, began filling with people. Others brought folding chairs and blankets.

The dancers entered single file, men then women and children—the tinkling vibration of a thousand sleigh bells like the rushing of a river. Excited singers and drummers reached a frenzied peak. The dancers moved right to left until a circle was formed, each dancer moving according to how the song moved, some as individuals, two-stepping, jumping, bending low to the ground, whirling around, a few contraries (an ancient backward-doing society) moving against the flow; others in groups, moving in rhythm—all a blur of bright color and movement accentuated by feathers and fringe and paint, as wild and eerie a sight beneath the halogen lamps as you are likely to see in Crow country these days.

I was sitting next to a German dressed like Sitting Bull. The German's face was painted black, and his costume was entirely of buckskin, his head topped by a huge warbonnet. He was sweating profusely and spoke in a thick accent. Germans have been fascinated by plains Indians ever since Karl Bodmer and Maximilian returned from the American West in 1834. The German belonged to an Old West Club. Several members were here. They had been far happier across the ocean with their Bodmer lithographs and fantasies. He said you wouldn't see these lawn chairs at a German Indian powwow. The dancing would have started promptly at eight. And all this litter. Achhhh.

"Everybody dance," said the announcer. "Everybody come and dance." And the people did, moving out of the grandstands, out of the dark, some dressed for the competition, many in their everyday clothes, men in Levi's and business suits, old men and women, children of all ages, some just old enough to walk.

As Native American dancers once assimilated the

things of everyday life into their dances, the motions and dress of animals, the bright colors of the earth around them, so they do today. There are traditionalists who imitate the old style, the dress and dance of the buffalo days, but an Indian dancer is just as likely to wear silken basketball shorts and striped gym socks with feathers and beads.

I listened and watched as long as I could, enjoying the beauty of what I was seeing but understanding nothing, not even the subtle differences between songs. Then I walked to my car and drove outside of camp and up into the hills until the lodges spread out below me. I watched the constant circling of the car headlights through camp. A dozen tipis were lit up from inside, the shadows of the occupants making dim pantomimes. Music rose into the night sky, and coyotes howled back and forth in answer.

The reservation police came within five minutes, questioning me, looking in the car with flashlights for beer and whiskey, illegal to have on the reservation.

They couldn't understand what I was doing up there. All the fun was down below in camp. That's where the women were. As they drove away I could hear them laughing. Dumb white man.

Five minutes later a pickup pulled up behind me. "Want to buy some wine?" a voice asked. "We got ice cold beer, dollar a can." No, I said, and they drove away.

Next, a man about my age materialized out of the darkness, came and leaned against the car with me, both of us silent for a minute, looking out, listening. His name was Steven and he was from the camp down below, the tipis closest to us. He was a painter. He wanted me to come down and look at some of his work, maybe buy something. Someday he was going to be famous like Kevin Red Star. "Man, that cat buys a new car every year." I said I didn't want to look at any paintings. He asked if I had any herb. "Man, I could sure use some herb." When I said I didn't have any herb, he said goodbye, stood silent for a long time, and then dematerialized back into the dark.

I pitched my tent on a grassy knoll on the fringes of camp, waking on and off. At 2:00 A.M. I dressed and walked down the road among the tipis. The competition dancing was over, but the drums and voices of the Forty-Niners were calling. Young people were drawn to them like moths, pressing closer and closer around the singers. The summer night was hot with the closeness of bodies, with people coming and going, moving here and there, all in street clothes, swaying to ancient rhythms, talking, laughing, all mingling into one unending pulsing of song and drum.

> *Yoeyo Yoeyo Aiii Yo hey yah hey ha . . .*
> *You're my one and only and I love you so dearly . . .*
> *Hey yah hey . . .*
> *Forever and eternally . . . Hey yah . . .*
> *Way nah ha way nah ha yo, hey ya, hey ya, hey ya . . .*
> *Tell me that you'll always love me and be true,*
> *   sweetheart . . .*

You'll know that I'll always love you . . .
Way nah ha way nah ha yo, hey ya, hey ya, hey ya . . .
Oh, my honey, you are the only one I check out at the
*   powwow I never notice anyone else . . .*
Hi hi hey ha yo ya hey way ha . . .
My one and only although you're living with another
*   one here . . .*
It's always only you I'm thinking of . . .
Someday our dreams will come true and then you'll
*   always be mine, be mine from now until eternity . . .*
Hi ya way hi ya . . .
Aoooo hey a way hi ya. Aoooo hey a way hi ya . . .
When we're together I feel so fine dear . . .
Love me tonight, dear, the time is right . . .
Yoheyyaway. Yoheyyaway . . .
Aoooo hey a way hi ya. Aoooo hey a way hi ya . . .
Darlin', I will see you tonight here . . .
At the Forty-Nine here, that's where we'll meet . . .
Hiya way ya. Hiya way ya. Hey way ohohh . . .

The Forty-Niners sang all night, and with the first
sunlight the people vanished. Around the drummers it
was as if a bomb had gone off—bodies everywhere, inside and on top of cars, lying asleep here and there,
standing in ragged clusters, reluctant to let the night go.
In front of a tipi across the road a couple stood wrapped
in a blanket facing the sunrise, rocking from side to
side.

Already the cryer was up and about, driving slowly
around camp in a pickup, yelling hoarsely in Crow over

a loudspeaker, urging the people to wake up, to get ready for the parade. In the old days the cryer would be saying something like this: "Make water come into contact with your body. Get up, drink your fill. This will keep your blood thin and you will not get sick. You will be active, your blood will not clog, it will flow through your veins. Water is our body. Whatever else there be, water is above all; without water you cannot live. If you use very little water, you will not live and enjoy life."

Smoke from cook fires began to rise. I could smell bacon. Already there was a line of people waiting at each plastic john. Others washed their hair or filled water jugs from spigots.

I drove up to the Custer Battlefield, parked the car, and walked down to the Little Bighorn, stripped, and jumped in. There had been a fire and the battlefield looked especially stark, the stone markers placed where men had fallen shining like white pebbles against the black earth. There are many stories about how Custer died, but the one I like best is that of an old Cheyenne warrior who fought that day. When asked what the battle was like, the old man spent several hours gathering twigs, peeling their bark, and sticking them in places, rearranging them many times to represent the placement of the troops. Then he took his hand and in one motion swept everything aside. Poof!

What must it have been like, to have looked down on the single largest gathering of the plains people, a vil-

lage of villages stretching for miles up and down the
Little Horn River, so many horses that the Crow scouts
mistook them for buffalo. "There are more Lacota than
the soldiers have bullets," they told Son of Morning
Star, but still he wanted to fight. "We are all going home
today," the Crow said, "but by a different path."

It is told among the Crow that Custer died in the
water at the ford, that he fell with his scout Mitch Boyer
in the water where I bathed, long before they ever retreated to the hill and the proverbial last stand.

I left Crow Fair and drove across the Bighorn Mountains to see my friend Dick Greeves. Dick lives among
the Shoshone and Arapahoe in a great rambling house
on the Wind River Reservation, his home since he ran
away from St. Louis at the age of fifteen. His wife Jerri
is Kiowa and runs the Fort Washakie Trading Company. Jerri's people came out of the earth through a hollow log in the mountains near where the Yellowstone
rises; her grandfather was a warrior who told stories of
raiding south into Mexico and returning with plunder.
Dick is a sculptor who dreams of wild gardens peopled
with his bronze spirits, of monuments to Crazy Horse
and Washakie.

I arrived just as Dick was leaving to take a sweat bath
with some friends. Everyone was already inside the
lodge by the time we got there, but the flap of the door
was still open and the heated rocks had yet to be put in.
A skinny white man with a bald head and mustache
was tending the fire. We stripped and entered, sitting

down cross-legged, completing the circle of men already seated. The lodge had thick earthen walls and a willow roof covered with a tarp. A bundle of eagle feathers hung by a thong just left of the entrance. Dick introduced me. Two younger men shook my hand. Others grunted. "MMMMMMhhhhh." "Ahuhhhh."

To my left was a man who'd attempted suicide by shooting himself in the mouth. Left of him, a small smiling man in sunglasses, and left of him, Harrison Shoyo, gray hair worn in a burr. Harrison had led the peyote ceremony the night before. The men had spent Saturday night fasting and dreaming, and now, they would be reborn in sweat. Eddie Shoyo had the place of honor opposite the door, where the heat would be most intense. Next to Eddie was Ben Shoyo, his long braids wrapped in green cloth. Next to Ben was a Uweepee medicine man, a young man in his early twenties; he'd been sent away to the Sioux to have his special gift developed when he was a child. Now the people take care of him.

Eddie spoke, a long monosyllabic speech, thanking everyone for coming and for the good ceremony of the night before. As he talked, the men grunted their approval of what he said. "Yes," they said. "Ahoe," they said. Then each man thanked Eddie for inviting him here, for building this good sweat lodge, for the good ceremony they'd had the previous night. "Good," they said. "Yes."

Eddie asked for the rocks, and the white man outside lifted them through the door with a shovel one at a time. The rocks had been cooking in a fire all afternoon and pulsed with red heat. Four rocks were placed in a hole in the center of the lodge's floor.

Eddie sprinkled crushed cedar leaves on the rocks, and each man leaned forward and passed his hands through the smoke, drawing it toward himself, touching his face, his arms, his legs, patting himself on the chest.

Eddie asked the white man to close the door, and it became as dark as a womb inside. I felt as if I were floating, unattached from the body that held me to earth. I could feel the men on either side of me, could hear them breathing. It grew hot, and the sweat began to come. Eddie said he was going to put the water on, and I heard it sizzle on the rocks and turn to steam. The air grew hotter. I felt as if I were breathing fire. Dick had told me that if it got too hot I should lean forward; the main thing is not to pass out and get burnt on the rocks.

Eddie thanked everyone again for coming, and everyone thanked Eddie. This new lodge was a good one they said, better than the one the river had washed away. Then Eddie called for the white man outside to open the door, and one by one we walked outside and down to the Little Wind River. We rolled over and over in the cold fast water. Then leisurely walked back to the lodge to stand and visit and dry off in the sun. "You're lucky Jimmy Stump isn't around," sneered the fire tender, "he likes to cook white guys. I come outa' there once with blisters the size of eggs on my back."

Eddie told the story of the fire. Once while the men

were in the lodge the fire outside got out of control. Inside it kept getting hotter and hotter but everyone thought it was just an especially good sign. No one wanted to go out. They were singing. When they finally did come out, the land around for five acres was burning. Firemen were there. "Those guys were surprised when we came walking out through the smoke in our swimsuits," Eddie said and everyone laughed. Harrison began talking to me, his words like a stream rising and falling in my head, swirling around and getting jumbled. He talked about the peyote ceremony, how it came to his people, what it meant. He talked about medicines and herbs, all the fine things the Indian received from the earth, and then Eddie called for us to come in.

Eddie thanked everyone and everyone thanked Eddie. More rocks were placed inside. We drank water, blessed ourselves with the smoke, and the door was closed. It was hotter and I felt my skin glistening with sweat even before the steam. It grew so hot I felt as if I were melting. There was a sweet smell. I was handed some sagebrush and brushed my body with it. The medicine man spoke. He thanked Eddie and each individual for coming. He had traveled a long way to be here. He was glad to be here among people who practiced the Indian Way. These eagle feathers he had brought had belonged to his mother. She had given them to him just before she died. She said for him to use them to help people. They possessed special powers. He would pass them around. In darkness the feathers traveled hand to hand. I held them and pressed them to my face, closing my eyes, then I passed them on. And then the medicine man began a high, keening yelp. Harrison spoke. This sweat was for his grandchildren who were going away to college, leaving the reservation and their family and friends, going into the white man's world. "Please watch over them," he said, "pray for them, help them make the right choices, bring them back home often to be among loved ones."

"Ahoe," said the men. "Yes. Good. Uhhhuhhhh."

Another voice spoke. "Please help me whip this alcoholism. I'm so tired of going down that road."

"Good," they said. "Ahoe. Yes. Yes."

"Help me with this diabetes," said another. "Give me the strength to fight it and get it out of my body."

"Uhhhhhuhhh. Ahoe. Good."

"Give me children," said another.

"Help my brother," said another. "Help him be happy with his life. Let him live a long time. Give him laughter and children and a good wife."

And then everyone was talking at once, talking in English, in Arapahoe, in Sioux, Ute, and Shoshone. Calm voices, weeping voices, beseeching voices, and the weird wailing of the medicine man all mingling like vapors in the dark heat. Was I dreaming? I was mumbling. I could taste the salt of sweat. And then Eddie called for the door.

I lay in the river a long time, on my back, looking at the mountains and sky, feeling the water wash over me, rising only when Eddie yelled that it was time to go back in.

Eddie thanked everybody and everybody thanked

Eddie. Harrison spoke. He thanked Dick for coming and taking this sweat. "You are one of us," he said, "you know our thoughts. You are my grandson's uncle. You have been helping him with the Indian Way. Now he must find a new way. I would like you to say a few words."

Dick thanked everyone present. He was thankful for this good life, for all these good things, for all his good friends here. He said children were like water and would find their own course. He would pray for them to find the right path, to make the right choices, to be happy. Then he turned to me. "I want you to know that this is how the Indian has always been. He has welcomed the white man, treated him like a friend. You know how the white man has treated the Indian." Grunts of approval.

"Ahoe. Yes."

Harrison looked at me. "This is true," he said. "You have been among us, you have sat in this lodge with us. This is the Indian Way. It is our religion. We live our religion every day. We hope that you will take good thoughts about our people and the Indian way of life with you on your journey. That you will tell your family good things about us, that you will write good things about us."

"Ahoe," they said. "Huuhhhh. Good." And then Eddie called for the door.

Pulling off the sandbar we drift down to an island below the Bighorn. I beach the boat, take my bag and pad and slicker into the brush, plop down, crawl in, curl up,

and fall asleep, waking now and then to the rumble of
coal trains crossing the bridge.

"this river below the big horn resembles the Missouri in
almost every perticular," wrote Clark, "except that its
islans are more noumerous & current more rapid, its
banks are generally low and falling in the bottoms on
the stard. Side low and extenecive and covered with
timber near the river such as Cottonwood willow of the
different species rose bushes and Grapevines together
with the red berry or Buffalow Grees bushes & a species
of shoemake with dark brown bark. from those bottoms the Country rises gradually to about 100 feet and
has some pine. back is leavel plains . . . on the Lard Side
the river runs under the clifts and Bluffs of high which
is from 70 to 150 feet in hight and near the river is some
scattering low pine back the plains become leavel and
extencive. the clifts are composed of a light gritty stone
which is not very hard. and the round stone which is
mixed with the Sand and forms bars is much smaller
than they appeared from above the bighorn and my
here be termed Gravel. the colour of the water is a yellowish white and less muddy than the Missouri . . .
    "Buffalow and Elk is estonishingly noumerous on
the banks of the river on each side, particularly the Elk
which lay on almost every point in large gangs and are
so jintle that we frequently pass within 20 to 30 paces of
them without their being the least alarmd. The buffalow are Generally at a grater distance from the river,
and keep a continuing bellowing in every direction,

much more beaver Sign than above the bighorn. I saw
several of those animals on the bank to day. The anti-
lopes are scerce as also the bighorns and the deer by no
means so plenty as they were near the Rocky Mountains
. . ."

No "buffalow" bellows, and there are no "jintle" elk on
the Yellowstone today. All the grapes were lost in a
freeze in 1936. But much is still unchanged since Clark
saw it.

The day clouds over soon after dawn. Wind brings
snow and sends me burrowing down into my coat.

A beaver swims out of a hole in the riverbank and
swims in circles around the raft, an oar length away:
gliding ahead, popping the water with a tail, diving
from sight, coming back to hover out in front or on the
sides—golden coat glowing in the sunlight, black nose
shining, web feet splayed. Stryder leans so far out over
the tubes trying to get a good smell he almost falls out.
After a while the beaver loses interest and swims back
upriver in the direction from whence he came.

At the height of the fur trade, a half-million beaver a
year were dying so that gentlemen could wear them as
hats.

According to Dick Greeves, this is how you trap beaver:

Beaver trap, good kind, has a double spring,
weighs five pounds, is attached to a chain with a

swivel. This is so that as the beaver spins, drowning, the chain don't kink.

You got to scout around, get the lay of the lodge, dams, and runs—if you're on a pond. Do this wading so your scent don't hang around. Wear rubber boots. Wading around in the ice water in moccasins is what crippled all them old mountain men. Pelts not prime in warm weather. Sometimes you can hear beaver inside the lodge if you put your ear to it—mewing and cooing—sounds like little kittens in there.

Now, set the trap in three foot of water and stake it through the ring at the end of the chain. You can drop the ring around a sapling if it's handy, or nail it in a log. Best to stake it. Do this near a run or spill. You can chip a cut in the dam and that'll make 'em come. Attach a float stick to the trap—there's lots of ways. Dab on a little castoreum. It don't take much. That's the musk from glands near the anus. Both sexes got 'em. Strong perfume. Sickly sweet. Medicine. Indian woman put a little bit on her throat. You can throw a handful of mud on the bank near the trap, put castoreum on, and catch a beaver putting his own on the pile. When he comes to take a whiff on the stick, he catches a foot, dives for deep water, and then it's over. Beaver can hold its breath for five minutes. Sometimes it takes a while to drown. Sometimes they chew off their own leg.

Skin 'em carefully, split up the legs and belly. Stretch the hide on a green willow hoop with leather or shoelace. It's worth about twenty bucks. Steaks are good on a beaver's backside. And you hear a lot about tail—if you're curious, roast it on a stick until it pops and grease sizzles on the coals. Likely you'll not find it the tastee-treat the old people did. Living on wild meat, you see, they didn't get much fat, which is what tail is all about.

Manuel Lisa came to St. Louis by way of New Orleans—a trader, shrewdest of the shrewd, an empire builder. He'd wrested a centuries-old trade arrangement among the Osage from the powerful Chouteaus and nearly aborted Frémont's expedition to the southwest by holding up their supplies because he desired the Santa Fe trade himself.

"Lisa we thoroughly detested and despised," wrote a contemporary, "both for his acts and his reputation. There were many tales afoot concerning villiany said to have been perpetuated by him on the frontier. These may have been wholly false or greatly exaggerated, but in his looks there was no deception. Rascallity sat on every feature of his dark complexioned brow."

He was called the Black Spaniard, spoke neither French nor English, and had a French wife who couldn't speak Spanish. It was Lisa who acted first on the knowledge Lewis and Clark brought home—he stooped on the opening of trade in the West like a hawk. When the ice went out the spring of 1805, Lisa's keelboats began pushing north, and were waiting, like fate, at the mouth of the Platte when John Colter came paddling his dugout around the bend fresh from his first winter's trapping.

Keelboats were built of oak and were about seventy feet long and eighteen feet wide. A low cabin sat in the center and on either side of it was a walkway the boatmen used when poling upstream. There were six oars to a side, a brass cannon on the bow, and a rudder in the stern. When neither poles nor oars nor sail moved the boat, the crew pulled it upriver by cordelle, pulled it over mudflats and through willows and quicksand. The men jumped into the water to escape bears, were ambushed and slaughtered by the savages, were sucked on by the mosquito hordes, and were drowned in the brown flood of the spring rise against which the boat was moved.

"Keelboaters," observed Mark Twain, "were rough and ready men; rude, uneducated, brave . . . heavy drinkers, coarse frolikers, heavy fighters, reckless fellows, every one, jolly, profane, bankrupt at the end of a trip, fond of boredom . . . prodigious braggarts, yet in the main, devout, trustworthy, faithful to promises and duty and often picturesquely magnanimous."

Most famous among the keelboaters was Mike Fink. "I love the wimmin'," he hollered. "I'm chock full of fight."

Fink's most dastardly exploit, in a career devoted to such, was the killing of John Carpenter in the spring of 1829 at Fort Henry at the Yellowstone's mouth. Carpenter, a man named Talbot, and Fink had wintered together somewhere on the Yellowstone. They had fallen into dispute, presumably over a woman, but decided to make their friendship good again. To seal the deal, Fink and Carpenter would shoot a cup of whiskey from each other's head, a favorite rite. Carpenter lost the coin flip—Fink would shoot first. Drawing a bead, Fink admonished Carpenter to "hold his noodle steady" as presently he, Fink, would want a drink—and then coolly shot him between the eyes. Some years later, in his cups, Fink boasted that he'd shot Carpenter on purpose and was glad of it. The avenging Talbot killed him with a pistol on the spot.

But that's getting ahead.

Lisa's men were French, hardy kin to the voyageurs who'd gone running over the portages with 180-pound packs for the Hudson Bay Company: engagés, laborers, a few former pirates and convicts outrunning the constable, swaggering Finks, and quiet, dangerous men. Lisa ruled them as a lion tamer would: cursing and praising and cajoling them with his burning Spanish every mile of the way, 15 miles a day, 2,100 miles up the Missouri.

Lisa wanted to set up a post among the Blackfeet near the Missouri's three forks, but Colter diverted him up the Yellowstone to the Crow. It was late November when they reached the Bighorn River's mouth and began building Fort Raymond. It was here that Lisa sent Colter on his famous winter sojourn in search of the Crow camps.

The rest of his men Lisa put to work trapping beaver. Using white trappers to secure beaver instead of the traditional reliance on trading with the Indians was a first in the West. But Lisa's instincts were right, and when he set off in the keelboat for St. Louis the next spring, he carried a substantial fortune in furs. He'd turned his $7,000 investment into $15,000 profit. If he'd been unable to find backers in his fur venture before, he had no trouble recruiting purses that summer, from William Clark, Pierre and August Chouteau, and Benjamin Wilkinson, and forming the Missouri Fur Company. In the spring of 1809, Lisa left St. Louis with thirteen keelboats and a hundred and fifty men.

That same spring John Colter set off with John Potts to trap on the Missouri's headwaters. Blackfeet surprised them. Potts was riddled and dismembered, the pieces flung in Colter's face. Rather than waste a man of Colter's stature with a simple killing, the Blackfeet stripped him and told him to run for his life. Colter ran until he bled from his nose and ears. He killed the closest warrior with the man's own spear, then jumped into the Madison River and hid beneath a logjam while his enraged tormentors howled and screamed and searched.

Colter arrived at Fort Raymond a month later, "nearly exhausted by hunger, fatigue and excitement," according to Henry James, "his only clothing was the Indian's blanket whom he had killed in the race, and his only weapon, the same Indian's spear which he brought to the fort as a trophy. His beard was long, his face and whole body were thin and emaciated by hunger, and his limbs and feet swollen and sore. The company at the fort did not recognize him in this dismal plight until he made himself known."

Lisa built trading posts on his way up the Missouri at

the mouth of the Platte and on Cedar Island. At the Yellowstone's mouth he took half of the crew and went to the Bighorn. A partner, Andrew Henry, headed up the Missouri to establish a post among the Blackfeet.

The post among the Crow flourished, but the Blackfeet were intolerant. Colter had earned their hatred to such a degree that the entire upper Missouri had been made unsafe. George Drouliard, Colter's friend and fellow Lewis and Clark expedition member, was found "mangled in a horrible manner, his head cut off, his entrails torn out and his body hacked to pieces" less than two miles from the Three Forks post. Ambush followed ambush and altogether twenty trappers died before Andrew Henry abandoned the country and fled overland to winter and almost starve on the Snake River.

There were other difficulties. The oncoming war with Britain and the British threat in the northwest put an end to minor empire making while war was prepared for and waged. The Cedar Island post burned to the ground, taking with it a winter's catch of pelts. By the spring of 1811, Lisa's partnership had dissolved.

"I go a great distance while others consider whether they will start today or tomorrow," he once said. "I impose upon myself great privations. Ten months of the year I am buried in the depths of the forests. Cheat? The Indians call me father."

Lisa traveled the Missouri no less than a dozen times, spent seven winters among the Indians, and yet when he died, at the age of forty-seven, it was in bed of a cold.

After Lisa's death, ownership of the Missouri Fur

Company went to Joshua Pilchner, who once again tried to establish trade with the Blackfeet. Seven of his trappers were ambushed and killed on the Yellowstone, and all their horses and $15,000 worth of furs were taken. Some said it was instigated by the British—a thousand of the pelts turned up at the Hudson Bay Company's Edmonton post. Pilchner was broken: "The flower of my business is gone." The Missouri Fur Company withdrew from the upper river trade and faded out of existence.

Nothing by way of fur ventures happened in the Yellowstone country until well after the War of 1812. In 1822, William Ashley and his partner Andrew Henry created the Rocky Mountain Fur Company and placed this advertisement in the *St. Louis, Missouri, Gazette and Public Advertiser*:

Wanted
For the Rocky Mountains
the subscribers wish
to engage One Hundred MEN
to ascend the Missouri
to the
Rocky Mountains,
There to be employed as hunters. As a
compensation to each man fit for such business,
$100 Per Annum.

William Ashley had been a general in the Missouri Militia who'd made a fortune as a munitions maker during the War of 1812. Henry had been with Manuel Lisa and knew the wealth to be wrought from furs.

But the Rocky Mountain Fur Company was plagued with foul luck from the start. One of the two keelboats struck a snag and sank with a total loss of cargo. The Assinoboines stole fifty of the horses.

Andrew Henry pressed on to the Yellowstone's mouth in the remaining boat. Ashley returned downriver for more supplies and recruits. He came back the next spring to find Henry, but ran into an Arikara ambush that saw the undoing of fourteen of his men.

"Before meeting with this defeat," wrote James Clyman in his journal, "I think few men had stronger ideas of their bravery and disregard of fear than i had but standing on a bear and open sand barr to be shot at from bihind a picketed Indian village was more than I had contracted for and somewhat cooled my courage."

Young James Bridger was there, Tom Fitzpatrick, Jedediah Smith, Bill Sublette, Mike Fink, David Jackson, Daniel Potts and Hugh Glass, soon to meet a grizzly bear. It was Glass who penned this letter to a dead comrade's father:

Dear Sir:
My painful duty is to tell you of the deth of yr son who befell at the hands of the indians 2d June in the early morning. He lived a little while after he was shot and asked me to inform you of his sad fate. We brought him to the ship where he soon died. Mr. Smith a young man of our company made a power-

ful prayer which moved us all greatly and I am per-
suaded John died in peac. his body we buried with
others near this camp and marked the grave with a
log. His things we will send to you. the savages are
greatly treacherous. We traded with them as friends
but after a great storm of rain and thunder they
came at us before light and many were hurt. I myself was hit in the leg. Master Ashley is bound to
stay in these parts till the traitors are rightly
punished.

Yr. Obd. Svt.

HUGH GLASS

A brief and ineffectual campaign against the Arikara resulted. After it was over, Ashley left for St. Louis
where he was to run unsuccessfully for governor.
Henry took the newly bloodied recruits back to the Yellowstone, losing Hugh Glass to the bear and eight more
men to Indians before he reached the Bighorn. The
trapping was good that winter, though, and it made
Henry's fortune. When he returned to St. Louis the
next spring, he retired and never struck out for the
Rockies again.

In 1825 Ashley initiated new procedures in the fur
industry: bartering for furs at an annual trading rendezvous rather than at fixed posts and transporting the
goods and furs in and out of the country overland by
packhorse. Free of the river's whims, the heart of the
West was opened to roving trapper bands who penetrated further into the wilderness than ever before. For

the next quarter century there'd be few valleys that wouldn't know a white man's print. The rendezvous made Ashley the wealth he'd always dreamed of, and in 1826 he sold the Rocky Mountain Fur Company to Jedediah Smith, David Jackson, and Bill Sublette, washed his hands of beaver blood, and quit the Yellowstone country forever.

In 1828 John Jacob Astor, king of the American Fur Company, built Fort Union at the confluence of the Yellowstone and Missouri as part of his bid to monopolize the northwestern fur trade. His ablest prince was Alexander McKensie, and beneath his ruthless hand Fort Union became the most prosperous post upriver.

McKensie was feared and respected by red and white alike and would stop at nothing to gain the market from any he deemed competition. McKensie forced William Ashley off the river and overland to his rendezvous. McKensie established a post among the Blackfeet, succeeding where everyone else had failed. McKensie built Fort Cass at the Bighorn's mouth in 1832 and captured the Crow trade. McKensie's specially commissioned steamboat the *Yellowstone* made Fort Union the head of navigation on the Missouri, the farthest upriver a steamer had ever come. With it he smuggled in Mandan corn for the still to ply the illegal whiskey trade.

"How fared the *Yellowstone?*" asked John Jacob Astor, "and what said the Indians of her."

"The natives along the river appear very much awed by the big medicine canoe with eyes," wrote George Catlin whom the *Yellowstone* had brought upriver to paint Indians, "some prostrate themselves upon the ground while others shoot their horses and dogs to appease the Great Spirit whom they believe to be offended . . . upon sight of us cannons [at Ft. Union] roared for one half hour amid the shrill yell of half afrightened savages."

Three years later McKensie's steamer, *St. Peter*, delivered the smallpox.

And it was McKensie who jumped first into the buffalo robe trade when the decline of beaver signaled the beginning of the end for the mountain man.

Past Allen Creek, Unknown, Edwards, Forty-six, Forty-five, Forty-four, and Alkali.

By noon I can row no further and put down on the mainland, set up the tent, haul supplies ashore, settle in for the night and prepare for winter.

I wake to the screech of a screech owl, the squawk, quack, and whistle of passing ducks, the high melancholy song of geese going south. Winter day. Cold and crisp. An inch of snow on the ground, ice in the coffee pot. Raft covered with a thin frosting.

Flocks of geese beat their way into the air ahead of the boat, lines of migrants moving overhead, thousands of disharmonic voices providing constant concert. Clouds of ducks: mallards, pintails, and goldeneye.

The river requires my undivided concentration, the channels numerous and complex, often riddled with snags or flowing to a dead gravel end. I must row constantly, no time to kick back with the pipe or write much.

Past Buckingham, Roach, Antelope, and Wyant Coulee. Past Muggins Creek, Box Elder, McDonald, Frozen to Death, Starved to Death, and Sarpy.

At the mouth of Big Porcupine Creek, while we're eating lunch, a pretty vixen yaps at Stryder from a willow patch but he pays no attention other than a sniff.

Just south of here, in 1859, Captain William Raynolds of the U.S. Topographical Engineers got his first view of the Yellowstone Valley: "of which over fifty square miles was visible, literally black with buffalo, grazing in an enormous herd whose numbers defy computation, but must be estimated by hundreds of thousands."

Raynolds' expedition had been brought up the Missouri by the steamers *Spread Eagle* and *Chippewa* and deposited at Fort Pierre, South Dakota. From there, the expedition was to make its way overland toward the headwaters of the Yellowstone and Missouri rivers. The official mission was to make maps and determine the best course for roads. Twenty thousand emigrants a year were pursuing the American dream on the Oregon and California trails, driving a hundred thousand cattle and half as many sheep. Brigham Young's Mormons were heading with handcarts toward Zion.

"To whom does this land belong?" asked the Unk-papa Chief Bear Rib of Raynolds at Fort Pierre. "I believe it belongs to me. Look at me and at this ground. Which do you think is oldest? The ground, and on it I was born. I have no instruction; I give my own ideas. The land was born before us; I do not know how many years. If the white people want my land, and I should give it to them, where should I stay? I have no place else to go. He [the agent] takes my words and puts them into the water, and makes other reports of what words I send to my great father. I believe there are poor people below who put other words in the place of those I say. My brother, look at me; you do not find me poor, but when this ground is gone then I will be poor indeed."

Raynolds told the chief that he was unquestionably entitled to the right of transit through the Sioux country by virtue of being an American citizen, that he was fully able to defend himself if necessary, and that the president would hold the entire Sioux nation responsible if he were molested, and would send soldiers to wipe it from existence.

After the meeting, Raynolds visited the chiefs, less formally, in an apartment in the trading house where "the indians were lounging about the room literally au naturel. They had discarded their gaudy vestments and barbaric trappings, and with these their glory had departed. A filthy cloth about the loins, a worn buffalo robe, or a greasy blanket, constituted the only covering to their nakedness. They were lying about on the floor in all conceivable postures, their whole air and appearance indicating ignorance and indolence, while the inevitable pipe was being passed from hand to hand. Dirt and degradation were the inseparable accompaniment of this scene, which produced an ineffaceable impression upon my mind, banishing all ideas of dignity in the Indian character, and leaving a vividly realizing sense of the fact that the red men are savages."

After Fort Pierre and the Sioux, Raynolds and party proceeded across the plains. Raynolds noted that there were scarcely enough trees "on the average, to furnish shade for a single person in each square mile . . . Civilized life could find no home in this region, and if the savage desires its continued possession, I can see no present reason for its disputing."

Near the Little Missouri River three large bull buffalo charged the expedition, "to the great alarm of one of the escorts, who dropped his gun, and raising his hands exclaimed, in all the accents of mortal terror, 'Elephants! My God! I did not know that there were elephants in this country!'"

On another occasion, as the expedition passed near a buffalo herd, one of the wagon teams started in full pursuit: "Probably," wrote Raynolds, "the first buffalo chase on record with a six-mule team."

They moved into the Yellowstone country late that summer, struck the Little Powder River, followed it to the mainstem, and then crossed the divide to the Tongue and crossed another divide to the Rosebud. Raynolds followed that stream down to the Yellowstone, searching, with the aid of his American guide Bridger, for Fort Sarpy. After abandoning Fort Cass, the American Fur Company had created Fort Sarpy and had moved it up- or downriver whenever the wood supply ran out or the Indian danger became too great.

Raynolds described Sarpy as a "primitive affair," but its bourgeois, Robert Meldrum, was "undoubtedly the best living authority in regard to the Crows, outside of the tribe, having spent over 30 years in their country, during that time visiting the regions of civilization but once, and on that occasion spending only 19 days in St. Louis." Meldrum had assumed Crow dress and habit and spoke their language perfectly, telling Raynolds that it had become more natural to him than his mother tongue, and Raynolds "noted the alacrity with which he ceased speaking English whenever an opportunity offered."

"These Indians," Raynolds wrote of the Crow, "are of much lighter color than the Sioux, and have a less savage and repulsive expression. . . . Like all Indians, they are importunate beggars, and about camp they take constant and the most disagreeable liberties, thronging into our tents, rolling their filthy bodies up in our blankets, and prying into everything accessible. . . . They have no ideas of chastity, and greater general degradation could be with difficulty imagined. . . .

"A Crow glories in his long hair, which is worn straight down the back, frequently reaching to the knees. This is filled with gum, forming a compact mass, and is generally dotted over with white spots of paint. . . . Only in cases of extreme grief—mourning for friends, & etc. is the hair ever cut.

"A more senseless display of grief, common among them, is to gash the forehead and allow the blood to

flow over the face, remaining there until worn off by
time or obliterated by dirt. . . .

"As among all savages, the women are the mere
slaves of the men, doing all the menial service. A case in
point caused considerable amusement in our party. A
young Indian, almost a mere lad, with a stout and fine
looking squaw wife, has pitched his lodge a short distance from camp, upon the opposite side of a small
branch of the river. In all their visits to camp the wife
carries her liege-lord upon her shoulders through the
water with the most obsequious devotion. . . ."

From Fort Sarpy, Raynolds moved his party up the
Bighorn toward winter quarters, where he'd later listen
to Bridger tell of the Upper Yellowstone's wonders.

On its return a year later, the expedition was once
more accosted by the Sioux:

"The Great Spirit has made this country for us," said
Little Elk, "and has put buffalo and game in it for us,
but the white men come and build roads, and drive off
the game, and we and our children starve. I love my
children as you white men love yours, and when I see
them starving it makes my heart black, and I am angry.
We are glad to have the traders, but we don't want you
soldiers and roadmakers. The country is ours, and we
intend to keep it. Tell the Great Father we won't sell it,
and tell him to keep his soldiers at home."

In his final report, published in 1868, Raynolds con-
cluded that: "The valley of the Yellowstone offers the
greatest advantages of any part of the country explored.
It is fertile enough to yield generously to the hand of the

farmer, and the capacity of its hills for grazing is unlimited. . . . There is every reason to believe that the mineral wealth of the mountainous portion is very great. I purposely discouraged any desire among those under my command to search for gold, but, in several instances small quantities of the sands of some of the streams were washed and found to yield gold. . . . A road connecting the Platte and the Yellowstone is easy and practical, but it must go round, and not through, the Big Horn mountains. . . . A road with easy grades could be made from the mouth of the Yellowstone to the head of the Missouri at a cost within reasonable limits, and a full supply of fuel, pine, and cottonwood timber, and possibly, coal, could be obtained. The valley of the Yellowstone would form a good continuation of a route from St. Paul to Fort Union, into Oregon and Washington. . . ."

Which was exactly the way the rail was laid when the iron horse pressed into the Yellowstone three decades later.

Forsyth, Montana. A two-bridge town named for General James Forsyth, who landed here while touring upriver with Grant Marsh in the *Far West*, 1875. Chiseled into a concrete abutment is a "HOWDY" from "TEX, KING OF THE HOBOS."

I'd like to pass through but must stop to portage a diversion dam. No way through this one, no channel going around.

Tucking the boat into a canal a dozen feet from

where water roars over the concrete, I stand up and jump for shore with the bowline, miss the bank by a foot and fill my hip boots. It's such a shock that I drop the line to grab at a rosebush and almost lose the boat.

Everything must be carried a hundred yards overland through brush, a stinking toilet-paper wasteland at the outskirts of a state park at the town's edge. I gag every trip, sloshing along beneath my load, not wanting to linger long enough to empty my boots or change clothes, wanting only to be back on the river, cursing the mud, the dam, my own stupidity for jumping, the highschool kids sitting in their cars, motors running, getting high, making out, stereos rocking at full amp.

In 1959 the Montana Power Company bought the town of Colstrip forty miles south of Forsyth and began making plans to strip coal and feed two mine-mouth power plants: Colstrip I and II. Colstrip had a population of twenty then. Eight thousand people live there now. Construction on Colstrip Units III and IV has recently been completed, producing 2 million more kilowatts a year and mining 19 more million tons of coal, sucking up an additional 35,000 cubic feet of Yellowstone water for the conversion.

When the mining began, the primary concern of opponents was whether or not the mined rangeland could be reclaimed. Fingers were pointed at the slag piles back East.

The reclamation man at Colstrip took me on a tour a year ago. We drove around looking at test plots. He said it was easy to make the coal companies look bad. A lot of people were into that. He hoped I wasn't. The track record of the coal industry was one of the blackest, but things were changing. Most people were opposed to the mining because they hadn't taken the time to find out the facts. There were ranchers on both sides, "and some of them had turned down lucrative deals. People so in love with the life-style they don't want to lose it." Romantics. Antiques.

The reclamation man had been raised on a ranch, had worked for the state Fish and Game Department before coming to work for the coal mine. "If there was coal under my parents' ranch I'd sure as hell let them mine it. You bet."

He said there had been low interest in Western coal during the 1960s, but when the Environmental Protection Agency passed regulations concerning the amount of sulfur particulate that could be passed into the air there was a stampede among industries to burn Western coal. Western coal is twice as low in heating units but has half the sulfur. "Unless there's some really big change in the field of alternative energy, we're going to be mining coal in the West for a long time. America needs the coal. It's only a matter of time until the land is developed. Ranchers with places on coal stand to make quite a lot of money from their leases. Coal is really quite a blessing."

He said in the native-range-type ecosystem there is a natural cycling that takes place. The plants use nutrients, and then when they die they put them back. In

reclaimed land you lose the benefit of that cycling in the
first few years and have to make up for it with fertilizer.
It cost $1,400 to reclaim one acre.

They were monitoring the groundwater flow
around the mine in thirty test sites. Watching to see if
there was any increase or decrease in the salinity or the
flow. He said even groundwater moving through old
spoils is potable. Disturbed aquifers reestablish themselves in the materials that take the place of the coal.

The air around the stacks was monitored and sam-
pled every six days. "Close to the stacks, the particulate
matter is high but as you get further out it becomes less
and less."

He said many of the mine workers came from the
area. People who otherwise would have moved out to
find jobs. "A lot of these people worked for the larger
landowners as hired hands, barely making enough
money to survive, couldn't ever get ahead. One of the
reasons the landowners are upset with the mining is because it took away all their cheap labor. Ranchers are
traditionally conservative people, used to the life-style
and afraid of changing it." End of tour.

But, of course, the problems with strip-mining coal
in the West don't end with reclamation. There are
problems with assimilating new people into the area,
especially in the numbers coal has imported. Trailerhouses spawn on the prairies without plan. There's not
enough water. The sewage plant can't handle it. Not
enough police. The schools are crowded. Teachers and
students quit to work for higher wages in the mine.

More alcoholism, suicides, murders, and rapes. Clashes between cultures as vastly dissimilar as the red and white ones of a century ago.

And what of the river? Its water is pumped, sucked, diverted, and dammed—depleted to fill the growing need. There are no trout to save this part of the river, no eloquent flyfishers to give testimony or turn their pockets out.

But that's localizing the Yellowstone's problems. There's acid rain falling in the Rocky Mountains.

It's almost sunset by the time I get the boat repacked and shove off. Make only five miles before dark. Not far enough. I put down on a desolate beach: the bank's rip-rapped with a line of car bodies in various states of decay, all the grass on top has been cropped to a desert by sheep. I spread the poncho beneath three cottonwoods, one cut halfway through with an axe.

During the night I awake to the quiet pad of feet in the dark, Stryder moving off to explore. I no more than lay my head back down when a dog howl of pain and surprise jerks me upright, one hand groping for the pistol, the other for the flashlight.

"Something's got the dog," I think, jumping into Levi's and moccasins, walking as fast as I can toward the snarling and snapping. By shining the light I finally catch the reflection of green eyes. Growling and slobbering, Stryder leaps up into the air, twists, and gets jerked abruptly back to earth, his right leg distended. Trapped!

176

He snaps at me when I come near. "Easy big dog," I say, straddling him, crooning and whispering, getting a hand on his collar, holding his body between my knees, pressing on the trap's double springs with my feet.

I pull the trap up by its wire roots and stake, throw it, clanking, into the river. Probe around with a stick for others.

There're no broken bones but the leg's sore, and Stryder limps back to camp, lays his head next to mine when I climb back into the bag.

I wake up to coyotes yapping and yowling. "Are they laughing at us, Stryder?"

Wake up again to the dog growling. Something in the tone chills my scalp, and rising for a look I see headlights coming across the pasture toward us. The trapper's come to check his trap.

This is going to be ugly, I think.

I push Stryder down and flatten myself out just beneath the beam. Fortunately there's no tent sticking up. The trapper leaves his motor running, looks this way and that, scratches his head, examines the ground, hitches up his pants, scratches his ass. Turns the motor off. Turns the headlights off. Smokes a cigarette.

It's getting gray in the east and soon he'll be able to spot us without a light. Is he thinking about tracking? Will he drive straight forward a hundred yards?

But he gets back in, starts the engine, backs up, and bounces across the pasture to home. More than likely he'll return after breakfast.

I pack the raft as quickly as I can, throwing things in.

Carry Stryder aboard—his leg's now swollen—push off and drift away in starlight on black water. Oars squeak. Stryder licks his wound. Out here in this darkness, any number of bad river dreams could come true, but I'm more afraid of what could happen on shore.

Halloween.

Dawn is slow. The river steams. Steam turns to fog. Cottonwoods on islands float by in smoky detachment. Snags appear like the heads of monsters swimming upstream. Unseen ducks move overhead. An owl hoots. A loon laughs. A dog barks. A tractor starts up. The Plains.

At the mouth of Rosebud Creek I tie up for breakfast.

A lot of people, red and white, died on this piece of river when the Sioux finally tired of talking, moved into the Yellowstone country, and took it from the Crow. There were many desperate encounters in this brush, in these coulees and draws.

There were atrocities on all sides. White soldiers paraded black-haired scalps. Red men were burnt at the stake. Some of the boys were fond of jokes and rigged rifle shells and cannon balls so they'd explode, put strychnine into biscuits and left them around for the heathens to find.

A Crow at Fort Sarpy—some say Plenty Coups—reached a hand out from beneath a blanket to shake a white man's hand. When the white man took the Crow's hand, it came off—the arm of a dead Sioux.

"We've got you now, Joe," the boarding-school-educated warriors yelled at whites in distress.

In 1868 the army sent Colonel William Carrington to the head of the Powder River to construct Fort Kearney as a deterrent to the killing of travelers and gold-seekers on the Bozeman Trail.

From September on, the post suffered constant menace. Two thousand of Red Cloud's Sioux were rumored to be encamped in the hills. The wood train was fired on every venture out the gate for fuel. Stray civilians and soldiers were picked off. Always there was the smoke of emigrant wagons burning. Yet Carrington never struck back. He wasn't that kind of officer. Which caused his swaggering second in command, Lieutenant Colonel W. J. Fetterman, to boast that with eighty men he could ride through the entire Sioux Nation.

On December 21, Fetterman got his wish and with eighty men charged to the relief of a wood train, disappeared over Lodge Trail Ridge—disobeying Carrington's explicit orders—and never came back.

Fort Kearney was left to defend itself with a hundred men, each with forty-five rounds of ammunition.

"Do send reinforcements," Carrington wrote, "I have had today a fight unexampled in Indian warfare. . . . promptness is the vital thing. The Indians are desperate; I spare none, and they spare none."

Portuguese Phillips rode the message through the

gates on Carrington's prize Kentucky thoroughbred toward Fort Laramie.

Fearing the worst, Carrington placed the women and children in Fort Kearney's powder magazine. Should Red Cloud come storming up the drifts and over the walls, he would destroy everyone. But Red Cloud, satisfied that the army had been taught something by Fetterman's massacre, gave the siege up and retired to a more comfortable winter camp. One of those who'd counted coup on Fetterman that day had been a young warrior named Crazy Horse.

Phillips—so the legend goes—rode nights and rested days, outwitted and outran the Sioux, and delivered the message Christmas Eve night, interrupting the officers' ball by collapsing against the door. Carrington's prize horse lay dead at the gate.

When the Great White Father's representatives met the Sioux at Fort Laramie the next spring, they said they'd withdraw the troops if only the Sioux would promise to behave. Fort Kearney was abandoned, and the Sioux fired it before the retreating columns were out of sight.

That same year, fresh from financing the Civil War, the entrepreneur Jay Cooke began pushing for a Northern Pacific Railroad route through the Dakotas and up the Yellowstone. A line had already been run from the Pacific east to Bozeman, and with the Indian troubles over the survey could be completed. Fighting Phil Sheridan took William Tecumseh Sherman's place as commander of the Army's Division of the Missouri. Sheridan had fought the Southern rebels and the southern plains devils and had his own form of Indian policy. Things had been too lax. In guarding surveyors, Sheridan saw a way to flex some might—the immense blue war machine that had chewed up the Confederate States could now point, open mouthed, toward Indian country.

The escort provided Jay Cooke's Northern Pacific engineers in 1873 consisted of 1,900 troops (George Armstrong Custer's cavalry), 250 wagons carrying supplies, and the steamer *Key West*. Lonesome Charley Reynolds was Custer's scout. Yellowstone Kelley—Kelley the Sphinx—supplied meat with his snakeskin-wrapped Sharps.

As the survey was being carried out, the Austrian bankers withdrew their subscription to the bonds, calling the railroad idea premature. Cooke fell, and the railroad dream was set aside for nearly a decade. The following summer Custer took his cavalry on an expedition into the Black Hills to look for gold.

In June of 1876 the Sioux gathered with the northern Cheyenne in a concerted effort to wash the earth of the white man for good. As many as ten thousand Indians were encamped in the valley of the *ets-pot-agie-cate* or Little Mountainsheep River.

That same month the Army of the West under the command of General Terry initiated a large campaign to forever clean the earth of Sioux and northern Cheyenne. Terry moved troops into the Yellowstone country from three directions. The infamous Crook with his cork hat and mule brought troops up from Wyoming. Gibbon and his infantry marched in from the east, and a young hot-headed glory hound named Custer brought his cavalry in from the west.

Custer arrived at the mouth of Rosebud Creek for a supply rendezvous with the steamer *Far West*, his old friend Grant Marsh commanding, on June 19. Gibbon was marching slowly and was still five days away. Unknown to anyone yet, Crook had been attacked on the upper Rosebud and sliced up by warriors under the leadership of Crazy Horse.

Terry's scouts brought news of a large Indian encampment between Rosebud Creek and the Little Horn River, within two days' striking distance. Custer was dispatched the next morning, his orders to proceed up Rosebud Creek, find the enemy, and wait there until Gibbon and Crook's forces could complete the surround. He was to attack only if it looked as if the quarry were fleeing. From the *Far West*'s deck, Terry admonished Custer not to be greedy. There would be Indians enough for them all.

"I mean a thousand devils," Sitting Bull said of that day in 1890, "the squaws were like flying birds; the bullets were like humming bees. . . . Your people were killed. I tell no lies about dead men. These men who came with the Long Hair were as good men as ever fought. When they rode up their horses were tired and they were tired. When they got off from their horses they could not stand firmly on their feet. They swayed to and fro—so many young men have told me—like the limbs of cypresses in a great wind. . . . our young men rained lead across the river . . . there were a great many brave men in that fight . . . shot down like pigs.

They could not help themselves. One by one the officers fell. . . . it is said that up there, where the last fight took place, where the last stand was made, the Long Hair stood like a sheaf of corn with all the ears fallen around him."

Curly, one of Custer's Crow scouts, cried all night long on his ride back to the steamboat. Muggins Taylor then set off for Fort Ellis with the news.

Grant Marsh had run the *Far West* fifty miles up the Bighorn to the Little Horn's mouth on the day the battle occurred, a feat of navigational skill unparalleled in steamboating. It was surpassed only by the run he made back downriver to Fort Lincoln carrying Major Reno's wounded. It took two days for Gibbon's infantry to arrive from the battlefield with the litters. The men worked by the light of bonfires that burned for three miles up and down the Little Horn. The wounded were placed on mats of grass on the deck, and Miles Keogh's horse Comanche, the only survivor of Custer's command, was given a special berth in the stern. At dawn, while the surgeon cut and men moaned, Marsh hurtled his steamer down the Bighorn to the Yellowstone and down the Yellowstone to the Missouri, rushing seven hundred miles in fifty-four hours.

"I have heard the women tell of their intense excitement when they heard *Far West*'s whistle blast," recalled one of Reno's men, ". . . and how they waited and waited for tidings, each afraid to tell her anxieties, til near midnight when, with heavy hearts, almost with sobs, they separated and went to their homes. My wife told me how she tossed with restlessness until dawn when she was startled from a doze by a tap on her window, and instantly exclaimed: 'Is my husband killed?' She was answered by a voice choked with emotion: 'No, dear, your husband is safe, and Mrs. Moylan's husband is safe, but all the rest are dead.'"

In Philadelphia the World's Fair had just been turned on by Edison's electric light.

Ellen Cotton ranches a hundred miles south of here, among the willows and pine hills of Four Mile Creek on the Rosebud Divide near the town of Decker and the state's largest coal mine.

Though the name Cotton is English, Ellen is actually a Scot and is related to the Forbes. She is a great-granddaughter of Ralph Waldo Emerson, whom she refers to as RWE. Her first husband was a composer who won the Pulitzer Prize. They lived in the woods of northern California then and drove to music school, a great wild bunch of them, in a 1934 Rolls Royce touring car. When they divorced they sold the car for eighty dollars. Her second husband, Bill, was a hay contractor in Wyoming. He died ten years ago, leaving her the ranch.

Ellen Cotton has blue eyes and white hair that falls to her cheekbones. She once told a lady who was admiring her hair that she used Tide on it once a month. Sometimes Ellen tosses her head in a way that is somehow reminiscent of a colt. She wears Levi's and a wool shirt, tennis shoes in the summertime, boots when she rides (L. L. Bean's insulated ones in the winter), and a scarf that she sometimes unties from around her neck and wears over her head.

When she first came to Montana there wasn't a paved road west of Nebraska; it was the middle of the Great Depression. The train passed one abandoned farmhouse after another, doors hanging open and swinging in the wind. The train stations were filled with Scandinavian farmers with hands as big as shovels and bottles of gin in their hip pockets, all of them leaving.

Ellen says that there are a great many disadvantages in not having been born and raised in the ranch country, that there are a lot of things she doesn't know how to do well. But there is the compensation of never taking the country for granted. The land is a constant source of wonder and beauty to her. She has some money on the side; the ranch isn't her total source of income. Critics say she doesn't have to struggle and work like the rest of them. She can afford to be opposed to the coal mining. But Ellen does struggle and work. Work hard. Last winter when her hired man left, she fed the cows with a team of horses. In the summers she has as many as fifteen kids around her place helping out, but during the winter she is often alone and prefers it that way.

Ellen lives in a red house surrounded by lilacs. Cow and horse skulls hang on the front porch. Inside there's a massive coal stove, a rolltop desk, two couches, and lots of tables and shelves, all full, piles of books and magazines everywhere—months-old copies of *Life* and *National Geographic*. Some of her lamp shades are made of coffee cans. There are cedar boughs over the doors. The walls hold photographs and magazine cutouts of racehorses and anything else Ellen or whoever has stayed with her has had the fancy to put up: crayon drawings done by her children and grandchildren, prints brought to her from Vietnam and Thailand by her son Mike, recent and ancient calendars, a litho of a Holstein cow. Four or five flashlights lie around with dog bones and mementos. On her kitchen cabinet is tacked a copy of the War God's "Horse Song":

I am the turquoise
warrior's son
On top of belted mountain
Beautiful horses slim like
a weasel
my horse has a hoof like striped agate
his fetlock is like a fire eagle
plume
His legs are like quick lightning
My horse's body is like an
eagle's plumed arrow
My horse has a tail like a trailing black cloud
I put flexible good on my
horse's back
The little holy wind blows through his hair
His mane is made of short rainbows
My horse's ears are made of round corn
My horse's eyes are made of big stars
My horse's head is made of mixed
waters
From the holy springs he never knows
thirst

My horse's teeth are made of white
skull
The long rainbow is in his mouth
for a bridge
And with it I guide him
When my horse neighs
different colored horses follow
When my horse neighs, different
colored sheep follow
I am wealthy because of
him
Before me peaceful
Behind me peaceful
Under me peaceful
Over me peaceful
All around me peaceful
peaceful voice when he
neighs
I am everlasting and peaceful
I stand for my horse.

Ellen keeps the radio on all night, waking and listening on and off. There is an old coyote that comes
through the yard sometimes in the night, and Ellen will
have to get up to let her dog pack out the door to chase
him, and then she will have to get up to let them all back
in, except for Calle who was hurt and had to spend a
year inside and has since not been able to tolerate the
house.

Ellen gets up at four, dresses, and goes outside to

milk—snow squeaking underfoot in the wintertime and the sound of milk squirting into the bottom of a metal pail at twenty below zero.

There are other chores, a young Red Angus bull gets hay, the stallion Safari gets a bale of hay and grain, a dozen cats get cat food. "You better get well, old cow," Ellen says to an injured occupant of one corral, "I nearly sold you last fall." And then walking away she says, "I'm probably going to have to shoot that old cow and let the coyotes have her."

"You wouldn't believe it," she says patting a horse, "but this horse has been a top polo pony. She was flown to England three times and played against Prince Philip. She was born here on the ranch. Her name is Snowflake."

At six Ellen cooks breakfast and drinks coffee out of a glass mug, watching the news on television. After breakfast the pickup is loaded with hay, thirteen bales the first trip and thirty-nine the second. Ellen drives while her help, if she has any, stands in back cutting the twine with a knife and scattering the hay for the cattle by kicking the folds of the bales off the tailgate.

At noon, on a winter day, unless there's something special to be done such as setting salt meal out, repairing a fence or gate, working on a tractor or truck, or getting in a stray or sick cow, the chores are over until dusk.

One afternoon last winter Ellen drove me into Sheridan, Wyoming, town to her, and forty miles from the ranch. She said she never tired of the drive, there was just too much to see. We drove on gravel for a while and then on asphalt and then on a new highway. We passed by sleek new steel power lines. Ellen said the power lines ran to transformers at the Decker and East Decker coal mines. A coal train was running alongside the power lines, cars bending out of sight around a hill, moving on. Ellen said that she had seen twenty-five coal trains all lined up in the depot at Gillette. We watched the draglines feed, booms swinging out over the slag piles, jaws opening up—wide enough to hold a bus—dropping, and taking a bite of overburden, lifting and swinging and dropping their loads, twisting above the pine hills. Men walking around outside the draglines looked like ants.

Ellen said the machines cost around $60 million and took two years to build. They had to be built on the spot. They moved forward and backward on tracks. No dragline ever moved more than a mile in its life.

Down in the pit created by the dragline a smaller shovel dug out the coal and filled trucks. Ten tons to a scoop. "We're probably driving on top of a hundred-and-fifty-foot coal seam," Ellen said. A solid stream of traffic was coming down the opposing lane. The shift must be about to change. She used to love driving and not seeing anyone else on the road or any lights off in the hills. "You can't do that now." She pointed out a hill and said it never used to be there. She pointed to another place and said there used to be a hill there. She said the Decker reclamation was looking good, but it was easier to reclaim this land than some, especially, she said, when they put so damned much fertilizer on it. And spent so much money. She was waiting to see how well the reclamation did during a drought. The native grasses lay dormant during a drought. The native grasses could get along without much water, had evolved through these plains cycles and climates for millions of years. The native grasses could sustain and thrive. It made her sad that the coal companies put out all those noble television ads saying how it was all going to work when they didn't really know. "I wish they would just say they didn't know."

Ellen's niece Birdie got a lot of the coal uproar started. Birdie worked for the *Mountain Eagle Newspaper* ("It Still Screams") in Kentucky where the strip mining had all begun. Birdie had gotten a copy of the "North Central Power Study" and called and read it to Ellen, saying, "You better pay attention to this, this is what's going to happen to you."

Ellen phoned her neighbors. The ranchers got together and started having meetings to discuss what was happening. They organized.

Ellen said that at first the coal companies came in and scared people. They said they had the leases. They had eminent domain. They owned the mineral rights. They offered fantastic sums of money to people who'd only known what it meant to break even. Sometimes they came in cars and sometimes they came in helicopters and sometimes they came in bulldozers.

Ellen and her friends erected a steer-hide sign beside the highway. The sign was branded with the message:

NATIONAL SACRIFICE AREA
The government recommends strip-mining
the divide north of here.
We landowners oppose:

(and then it was signed with the branded names of the
opposing locals)

LET FUTURE GENERATIONS JUDGE

Some of those people are dead now. Some of them
sold out. Ellen doesn't blame them for selling. Ranching is a tough business to make a living in. "Times are
hard and getting harder all the time."

In Sheridan she showed me "all the ugly buildings
coal money built," and then we turned around and
drove back. It was storming and would be dark soon.
But as we drove, the storm wore itself out, and by the
time we passed the East Decker mine the night was
clear. The draglines were lit up and digging. Ellen said
they went twenty-four hours a day. "The first time I
saw the glow from the mines I thought the whole country over that way was on fire."

That night after supper I walked up the hill behind
Ellen's house and sat looking out over the valley. The
yellow light of Ellen's kitchen window spilled a small
pale square on the snow. The stars were dense and close
overhead and in the distance there was the faint tung-
sten halo of the mines. The sound of Pachelbel's Canon
in D wafted from Ellen's stereo between pine sighs into

the night. Ellen at the window, looking out, humming to it before going to bed.

Past Coal Creek, Iron Jaw, Graveyard.

Fewer islands now, fewer channels. The river's a quarter to a half-mile wide, calm as a lake. I bake in the sun, row, and spend the day counting eagles. Six so far. Geese and ducks as well; sandhill cranes high above, their voices a constant metallic belling. I become so enchanted counting cranes that I nearly run the boat onto snags twice. Three hundred birds are in one flock, six hundred in another. Flock after flock. Birds pouring down out of Canada, bound for the Gulf.

Past Snell Creek, Theade, Wilson, and Whitetail.

Drifting mostly. Stryder occasionally stirs to nurse his paw. Once, in a dream, he starts yelping and jerking his foot.

In the distance I can see badlands, the big broad empty. My main task, afternoons, is deciding where to sleep. An island with the proper view and exposure, shelter in case of a storm, sand to sleep on, a good beach to land on. Plenty of firewood.

At dusk a small red plane buzzes me, dipping so close, coming downriver, that I nearly abandon the raft. The pilot gives me a wave and grin. I shake my fist.

The drone lasts for a long time in the quiet, and the day's only made whole again by coyotes howling. Stryder doesn't stray far from camp.

Before light I wake to the damp of frost on top of the sleeping bag. A startled buck deer sneezes somewhere off in the brush, a sharp blast of air through nostrils. Fingers of mist swirl about the cottonwoods, rise off the river. The grass is delicately frosted—Stryder, too. Waking, he shatters his white coat and stretches.

As I pump up the boat—cold air shrinks it, probably a leak somewhere as well—my breath freezes on hair sticking out from my cap.

I shove off and meet the current. The sunrise turns the river mist to dense fog: white, like smoke, all around. Hoary old snags burble. Sweeper leaves tremble and brush the current. Mallards flush, quacking. Heron wings swish above. Water runs over gravel bars, against undercut banks, over sand and rock bottom— each playing a different tune. A creek roars in. Bluffs crumble into the water. Big splashes. Water laps at the banks. Eddies spin. Fish feed. Belly flop smack of a breaching sucker. Beaver tail slap. Silt scratches the raft's bottom. Squeak and creak of oars.

A coal train rumbles like thunder on tracks next to the bank, its great cyclops eye throwing a beam of light upriver, missing me. The wind of its passing makes a hole in the fog. It wails once, then it's gone.

Sunlight touches the river in rays, turning the fog orange and then yellow, touching me in warm light. For an instant I'm inside a cloud, glowing.

Past Cottonwood Creek, Swede, Steiger.

A duck hunter crouches behind a log, his decoys bobbing in the pool out front, looking so unnatural I spot them for fakes right off. But I don't tell him that.

"Hello," he hails. "Seen any ducks?"

"No," I say. "You?"

He shrugs, shucks a shell out of his gun onto the ground.

"Must be gettin' close to a town." Me.

"Yep. Miles City. 'Bout ten miles down. Where ya headed?"

"The Missouri."

"The hell." He gives a long appreciative whistle. "Where ya comin' from?"

"Yellowstone Park."

"The hell." He spits a stream of tobacco juice. "Guess you've seen some weather. How long ya been out?"

"If this is November first," I say, playing it up for all it's worth to his land-bound soul, "then I've been out twenty days."

"Hell. You know, another feller came by here not two months ago. He was from Livingston. They was a write up in the paper about him. He was in a log dugout, said he'd carved it out hisself, had a dog with him and a backpack. Was goin' to New Orleans. To a job down there if I recollect. Said he rolled over pretty regular till he got the hang of it."

"The hell," I say, having picked up his habit. And then I've floated far enough away that we can't do anything but yell, so we don't say any more. I lift my hand and he does too, then he disappears behind his log and I around a bend.

Past Moon Creek, Lignite, Reservation, Coal, and Cottonwood.

Twin brothers hail me next, seventy years old at least. Fishing.

"What you catchin'?" I yell through cupped hands, standing.

"Oh, pike, sturgeon, catfish," one calls back.

"The sturgeon's Cooneville sturgeon," hollers his twin. Must think I'm a biologist.

"How far to Miles City?" I ask.

"'Bout ten miles."

Next some folks in a motorboat pull alongside. They're catching the same thing. "This pool you're floating over is sixty feet deep."

"How far to Miles City?"

"Ten miles."

At noon we reach the muddy Tongue River, coming in on the right. I row up it a short way and tie the boat to a cottonwood tree with a wood sign nailed to it:

Swimmers Beware
Treacherous Waters.
Placed in memory of John Ewing '24'
Swept away and drowned
August 12, 1977

I've little desire to visit town, but must. I'm out of coffee, bread, and shells. There should be a package for me at the bus depot. I leave Stryder tied to a D-ring, guarding the boat, and walk down a dirt road toward the city.

Jim Bridger spent the winter of 1855 here with Sir George Gore, an Irish nobleman come west to have a sporting good time. Sir George's party traveled in six wagons: one for his arms—seventy-five rifles, a dozen shotguns, and a chest of pistols—two for his fishing tackle and flytier, one for his bedroom, and two for meat and camp gear. There were also twenty-one carts, twelve yoke of oxen, one hundred and twelve horses, fourteen dogs, forty servants, a brass bed that could be taken apart, a striped linen tent, a portable iron table and washstand, and the very best of wines. Sir George never loaded his own gun.

At night he read Shakespeare to Bridger, whom the mountaineer "rekined'd was too highfalutin' to suit him." Bridger "calcerlated that thar big Dutchman, Mr. Fullstuff, was a leetle too fond of lager beer" and thought it would have been better for the old man if he'd "stuck to burbon whiskey straight." Bridger was doggoned as well "ef he swallered everything that thar Baron Münchhausen said," and thought that some of his own adventures would be equally marvelous "if writ down in a book."

Sir George spent three years in the West, killing 2,000 buffalo, 1,600 deer and elk, and 105 bears.

From here he had flatboats built and floated down to Fort Union, where, in a rage over how much the American Fur Company was going to charge him for the trip home by steamer, he burnt everything in a bonfire—carts, harnesses, wagons, tents—and threw the leavings in the water. He made presents of guns to the Indians, gave food and livestock to some of the fort's workers, stepped aboard the steamer, and never came back.

· · ·

The year after the Custer fight, the army constructed
Fort Keogh near the Tongue River's mouth. Keogh had
been an officer in the Seventh Cavalry. Though his
horse Comanche had survived the battle, Keogh had
not.

Milestown, or Miles City as it's known, blossomed
close by to furnish the soldiers with stores and whores
and bars. The town was named for General Nelson
Miles, Keogh's commandant, who'd brought the Fifth
Infantry up from Fort Leavenworth to fight the Sioux.
The Fifth had been given the name Walkaheaps by the
Kiowa, whom they'd bloodied down in Indian Territory. It was the Fifth under Miles that put an end to the
Nez Percé's flight in 1874 when they caught Chief Joseph short of the Canadian border and pounded the
women and children into red meat with artillery. Miles
called the Nez Percé War "the greatest little Indian
fight ever."

Miles was an efficient officer, a practical, ambitious
man with his own ideas about how to wage plains warfare. He struck out from Fort Keogh with the same fury
he'd used on Red River. He sniffed the people out like a
hound. In Kiowa land the men of the Fifth had cut
their own arms to wet their lips with blood to stave off
thirst. To fight the Sioux, they lost feet and hands to
frostbite, froze to death on sentry duty or in their sleep,
suffered blizzards, never resting, never letting the people rest, ambushing them in their winter camps, as they
slept or made meat, drove them starving into the snow,
made ashes of all they left behind and killed their precious horses by the thousands.

The Sioux thought Miles was Custer's brother.

"I mean," said Sitting Bull, "that he had no caution."

Under a flag of truce Miles met Sitting Bull and demanded surrender. Sixteen hundred of the vanquished were herded aboard the steamers *Eclipse* (Grant Marsh in the captain's tower), *Josephine*, *Helena*, *General Terry*, and *General Sherman*, and sent downriver to the reservation. The steamer captains thought so lightly of the matter that they held a race. But Tatanka-Iyotanka and his warriors, vowing to fight to the bitter end, fled to Canada.

When the white man landed on the continent there were between 15 and 20 million buffalo, a black carpet of wooly humps all across the plains. In the spring the rivers stank of the buffalo death brought down on their floods. The Indians had depended upon them for ages, had created a way of life around them, attributed life to them. For a brief time after the horse, the people and the buffalo lived in great harmony; you can see that by the art, the dances and songs and words, and by the way they dressed, said prayers, and made offerings to the buffalo.

It took 8 to 10 buffalo hides to make a lodge, at least that many for clothing, and several to sleep in, not to mention those killed for meat. The northern plains tribes killed some 300,000 animals a year simply to survive. But that was far less than the herd's annual increase.

But once the Great Waste began even the Indian cashed in his god for profit. George Catlin describes a band of several hundred Assinoboines and Mandans crossing the Yellowstone ice near Fort Union and returning a few hours later with 1,400 buffalo tongues, which they exchanged for a few gallons of McKensie's rotgut whiskey. Then the robe trade began. Where once a man's wealth had been horses and counting coup in war, now it became material goods, guns with which to kill enemies, cloth and pretty things for the women, iron, powder, and lead, axes and knives not made of flint.

Two hides made one robe. Since making robes was woman's work, polygamy became the preferred way— simple economics—the more women, the more robes.

The Crow once lost a huge pile of robes in a horse racing gamble with a white man. Ho!

The transcontinental railroad split the one vast buffalo herd into halves, a northern and southern. There were close to 4 million buffalo in the southern herd, most of them in Texas, and 1.5 million in the northern, from the valley of the Platte north to Great Slave Lake, and west from the Dakotas to the Rocky Mountain foothills. By 1875 the southern herd had ceased to exist, and the hunters came trickling into the Yellowstone country like wolves trailing an injured thing.

General Sherman said every buffalo hunter ought to be given a medal: Every buffalo killed was one less an Indian would eat. Annihilate the source of life—break the people's spirit. He'd learned a few things marching through Georgia.

Hides were worth three dollars each, four-legged gold pieces just waiting for a man to pick them up.

Men left jobs and businesses, left wives, children, and friends, came to Miles City and bought one of Christian Sharp's guns—a 45-120, say, or a big 50—a twenty-power scope, two wagons, and a camp outfit and went to running buff.

A man killing a hundred animals a day could earn a profit of $6,000 in a month, and 10,000 hunters, skinners, drivers, cooks, and camp tenders began the business of converting flesh to cash.

In the end, none of it came easy. Hides spoiled. The buff spooked. You couldn't find the herds. Indians raided. A man carried poison for himself rather than be taken alive—the Sioux had special tortures for buff hunters. The weather was a hardship, November to March.

One old hunter said he'd spent ten years on the plains running buff (took 369 hides with 400 cartridges once), and all it'd netted him was 2,000 bucks. Friends said he was one who had gotten the most from it.

Once Indians came into camp and took everything, burned his and his partner's whole winter's mound of hides, said if they were around when they came back they'd kill the boys, gut shooting his partner to make the point clear. Why they just didn't kill them both he said he'd never know.

He set off to Miles City afoot to fetch a wagon and haul his partner into town. A chinook wind warmed the snow, and he broke through at every step, wetting his legs to the waist. When night came the temperature dropped below zero. If he'd quit walking, he'd have frozen. By and by he found a hole in a cutbank and crawled inside to sleep. He woke with rattlesnakes crawling all over him, warmed to life by his body heat, but not thawed enough to strike.

Rested, he set off in daylight, borrowed horses, and came back to camp.

Another time he and four others were caught in a stampede—the thunder of thousands of buffalo hooves shaking the ground, dust billowing in a thick cloud. They lay beneath the wagon, concentrated their fire on the herd's center, and split them around either side.

He'd once spent the night in a blizzard wrapped up in green hide and had to cut his way out with a knife the next day.

"Maybe we hunters were just a part in the natural progression of things," he recollected. "That the buffalo had to go. Or maybe it was just greed and we glad to get out of it all we could and keep our scalps on. Maybe that's the way it was."

In 1876 there were a half million buffalo within a hundred and fifty mile radius of Miles City.

"Most of our citizens saw the big load of buffalo hides that the *C. K. Peck* brought down last season," reported the *Sioux City Journal*, "a load that hid everything about the boat below the roof of the hurricane deck. There were ten thousand hides in that load, and they were all brought out of the Yellowstone on one trip."

Prior to 1880 only the prime, winter, Indian-dressed robes were used in trade. After that though the summer hides, green, cow, calf, and bull, were being used to make leather for the belts and straps turning the pulleys of the machine age.

By 1881 the Northern Pacific Railroad had pushed up the Yellowstone to Miles City. Its first payload was 50,000 hides. That was the year Vic Smith killed 107 buffalo in one stand; his total kill for the season was 5,000 animals.

In 1882 the railroad shipped 200,000 hides. That was the year a herd of 75,000 buffalo crossed the Yellowstone above Miles City, holding a steamer up for hours. Fewer than 300 escaped the line of gunners waiting in camps to the north. The army was issuing free ammunition—they didn't want the herd to reach Canada and feed Sitting Bull.

The next autumn the hunters all outfitted as usual, but came back with empty wagons after one month or a few. Not a carload of hides, not a pack, not one prime cow or bawling calf. Everyone thought the herds were just somewhere in the north, as if totally unaware of what had happened.

In 1886 William Hornaday, startled at the buffalo's sudden disappearance, made a search for specimens to be mounted in the National Museum. He left Miles City and was gone two months. He returned with twenty animals, most of all that were left between the Great Porcupine and the Rio Grande.

Next came the boners, gathering bones by the ton, shipping them east to be crushed into fertilizer. Then came the wolfers with their strychnine bait, and the cattlemen with their spotted cattle.

Cattle had been pouring up the trail from Texas and across from Oregon to fatten on the gamma grasses since the 1870s. The buffalo's demise made more range. By 1883 there were twenty thousand head grazing at the head of Great Porcupine; seventy-five thousand on the Tongue, and ninety thousand on the Powder, and Miles City drew every cowboy within ten thousand square miles.

"The town struck me as something new and novel," a cowboy reminisced, "two-thirds of the habitations being of canvas. Immense quantities of buffalo hides were drying or already baled, and waiting transportation. . . . Large bull camps were encamped on the outskirts of the village, while many such outfits were in town, receiving cargoes or discharging freight. The drivers of these ox trains lounged in the streets and thronged the saloons and gambling resorts. The population was extremely mixed, and almost every language could be heard spoken on the streets. The men were fine types of the pioneer—buffalo hunters, freighters, and other plainsmen—though hardly as picturesque in figure and costume as a modern artist would paint them. For native coloring, there were typical specimens of northern Indians, grunting their jargon amid the babble of other tongues; and groups of squaws wandered through the irregular streets in gaudy blankets and red calico. The only civilizing element to be seen was the camp of engineers, running the survey of the Northern Pacific railroad.

"Tying our horses in a group to a hitch-rack in the

rear of a saloon called the Buffalo Bill, we entered by a rear door and lined up at the bar for our first drink since leaving Ogalalla."

The "girls" followed the drovers cowtown to cowtown, working the circuit: Dodge, Abilene, Cheyenne, Deadwood.

"You know there was a kind of fascination in it," recalled one. "Hardly any of the girls would have quit."

Miles City was said to have drawn the prettiest. The Forty-Four was an infamous house here. Cowboy Annie had a brand book with all her beaus inside. Connie Hoffman was taken to England and made a gentleman's wife. Connie the Cowboy Queen had a dress embroidered with the brands of all the outfits her sweethearts rode in; it's said there wasn't a brand missing from the Yellowstone clear south to the Platte and as far east as the Little Missouri. Even Calamity Jane cribbed here occasionally in her younger days.

"The hotel accommodations in Miles City were not first class," rancher Grandville Stuart wrote in 1880, on a swing through Montana looking for cattle range. "In fact, I do not think there were any hotel accommodations. The people that frequented Miles City in those days usually came to town to stay up nights and see the sights. They did not feel the necessity for a bed or much to eat. They were just thirsty."

Miles City today: flashing lights, traffic. So much noise and color and movement all at once that I'm stunned, reel like a drunk on the pavement. I cross the street against the flashing neon "Don't Walk"—car horns blast me out of the way, tires and power brakes squealing. Good, smiling citizens part around me on the sidewalk. Coeds from the junior college scurry past without a second look. Dressed-up rancher families and businessmen going to lunch stare. A police cruiser goes slowly by, the cops inside giving me the evil eye. All towns look the same now, it's the homogenization of the range.

There's a package from Alisa at the bus depot, and while the station master sorts through boxes I fill my pockets with free matchbooks.

"Must be going to build a big fire," she says, eyeing my handful.

"I'm going down the river," I say.

She jumps back from the counter as if I were a snake coiled to strike. Her face pales, and she bites her lip, about to cry. "My brother drowned yesterday."

I nearly run back to the raft. Stryder is so thrilled he barks, something he rarely does.

A mile down and we meet a sobering sight: a half dozen motorboats full of grim men from the sheriff's department are dragging the river, tossing out massive trebled hooks, trying to snag a body.

"Duck hunter," one of the men informs me. "Turned over in a canoe and didn't come back up. Guess his hip boots filled up. No life jacket. Couldn't swim."

"That was foolish." Me.

"Happens all the time," says a deputy.

"Last spring a carload of kids went off a bridge. We

205

found the car three miles down the river. One body washed up on an island near Glendive. Never did find the others. I'll tell you what, I grew up around this ol' Yellowstone and I stay away from it. You watch out, or we'll be a fishin' for you, too."

A man in a motorboat, hovering below the searchers, roars over to pester me with questions.

"Zat one of them Arevon rafts? You pickin' up agates? Caught any fish? Shot any ducks?"

But I'm unable to relate, don't speak, and he buzzes on.

Past Kircher Creek, Bensley, Alkali, Sunday, Jones, Kelly, House, and Sand.

At dusk we drop through a set of waves. Buffalo Rapids, named by Clark, responsible for many a steamer's death. Not every pilot was a Grant Marsh.

I beach the raft just down from them, hoping they'll kill any city noise, and build a fire by lantern light. Eat supper sitting in the boat.

This morning I kill a cock pheasant in the willows and eat him for breakfast. The river's nearly a quarter mile wide, slow, like one long pool. We pass from cottonwoods onto the plains, dun-colored dirt banks on either side, gumbo and grass stretching to all horizons. Prickly pear and tumbleweed country; bluff and coulee country. Lines of wind-crooked trees mark distant creeks, clinging to life wherever there's enough moisture. When I stand up I can take in the long view—the Big Empty, puffs of dust knocked up by antelope hooves, white rumps flashing like mirrors. Now and then a coal train creeps across the space, sometimes a ranch house or ruined cabin comes into view. Dull, far-away gunshot thuds. Hunting season.

Past Spring Creek, Muster, Dixon, Deep, Short, Hay, Harris, Dead Horse, Cabin, Cottonwood, Sagus, Mack, Williams, and Camp.

A tram, bucket-shaped, rolls across the river on a cable above the raft. Someone inside waves and I wave back.

In the afternoon the blue sky clouds over. The wind brings snow, and I'm suddenly back into wool pants, shirt, and overcoat, earflaps on my cap tied down under my chin. Rowing into a storm. The horizon turns gunmetal blue, and there's a wild animal noise in the wind that I haven't heard before. It makes me afraid, makes me want to fly away or run or snug up in a den.

Stryder paces inside the boat, walking stern to bow, looking off, curling up, rising, walking bow to stern, and doing it all again.

Is this the storm that brings the ice? That finishes the trip? And what'll I do then? Walk to a ranch house, call home, and quit? I always knew it could happen this way.

Within an hour there's no more thought of finishing the day. I'm caught in the teeth of a true norther. It's so cold that tears streak uncontrollably from my eyes. The wind blasts my breath away. Water freezes on the oars.

No islands, no trees, no firewood, no backwaters, no breaks in which to fort up and hide. But a short distance up a dry creekbed I find the ruins of a dugout: a hole in the ground with a dirt-covered roof, three withered Russian olive trees for a windbreak, and a rusted stovepipe making strange music as wind howls over its lip.

I drag the raft as far onto shore as possible, moor it to a sagebrush, cover it with a tarp, and carry what supplies I'll need up to the dugout.

"Home," I say to Stryder, then I twist the knob and walk in just as if it were. The house is filled with tumbleweeds that I have to throw out. A crippled table and bed, a broken-down stove, broken glass, a spent shotgun shell or two, and bits of paper shredded for a rat's nest. But it's better than a tent.

Outside, I gather wood scraps from the remains of a dump. Rusted cans, odd bits of junk metal, a buggy seat, rotten chunks of harness, a horse collar, and a wagon wheel. I pump the well handle a few times, clacking and banging iron rods deep in a dry hole. Stryder jumps a big white-tailed jackrabbit, mottled brown and white, caught between winter and summer coats. The jack lopes gracefully just out of dog reach until both are dots, speeding off, despite my yells, curses, and stones. A second jack, all white, gets up and stops on its haunches, looking at me with a green eye, black-tipped ears twitching. I shoot him with the pistol.

Back inside, I roast a leg and quarter the rest for stew. Stryder paws at the door, slinks in, and collapses in a heap panting. Snow sifts in through cracks in the roof. I fall asleep trying to imagine who must have lived here and what it was like. What dreams they must have had.

Dirt underfoot, dirt overhead, dirt turning to mud all around. Wind and wolves howling. Baby crying. Did they grow to meet the space or did it make them small?

By morning, snow lies around in piles on the floor, like salt. The door's drifted in. It's gray outside, the wind's still blowing. I build a small fire to heat the stew, frozen in its pot. Hear a pickup coming my way. Then a metal door slams. A knock on the door.

"Oh no," I think, "here's the landlord."

A grizzled old rancher sticks his head in, cigarette dangling from the corner of his mouth. He snorts, seeing me and the dog. His name's Dan Haughians. He was out checking his bulls and saw the boat, the smoke. Before pickups, a man used to live in this dugout watching over the cattle, feeding them hay with a sleigh and team of horses.

Dan says he's seen the time when it's been mighty cozy in this little shack. I say it's pretty cozy right now, better than out on the river, which makes him laugh.

He says there were forty or fifty homesteads on his ranch, a homestead anywhere there was water. Used to be more people living in prairie country than there are now.

Dan has watery blue cattleman's eyes and a coarse Irish voice. He wears all the droughts, wind, good times and bad, the blizzards and hot plains sun of seventy-five years on his face. He's a bit stump-legged from riding all those jolting colts. His white hair's tucked beneath a flap-cap, one flap up, the other down. He wears a green plaid wool shirt, the pockets bulging with various pairs of eyeglasses and cigarettes. His Levi's are patched. He's got on overshoes. A good friend of his died this morning, had gone out to see his cattle and hadn't come back. His daughter-in-law went looking and found him sitting dead in his pickup with cattle all around.

Dan's middle son, Terry, is gone, rodeoing in North Dakota. Quinn, the oldest, and Pat, the youngest, are on a cattle drive, helping some neighbors up north.

Dan Senior, Dan's dad, left Ireland for the African diamond mines and stayed until the Boers drove him out. Then he went to Mexico, nearly got killed in the revolution, and fled to Oregon. In Oregon he bought sheep and trailed them to Montana—the drive took two years—staked a claim on forty acres, built a log cabin, imported his wife Susan from the mother country, and began raising lambs and wool. One time while Dan Senior was out fixing fences, a man came riding up on a lathered horse.

"McKinley's been shot!" the man yelled.

"McKinley?" Dan's father said, "Who the hell's that?"

Dan Senior died in 1931, leaving Susan with five boys, five girls, the start of a ranch, and the beginning of a drought.

On his deathbed, Dan Senior told Dan to take care of the family, to keep it together.

Susan had been an Irish beauty in her day, a gentle woman who'd not baked or cleaned or washed a dish before coming to America. In time she could ride as well as any man. She had a sharp business acumen and a quick mind; by her wits and the boys' strength she made the Haughians' ranch one of the largest in the state. She was courted by *Life* and *Look* magazines and was always here and there in the newspapers. She was fond of wearing long riding skirts and fringed shirts.

There were two years of little snow and hot summers, and the grass burnt up. In 1934 the grasshoppers came, so thick you couldn't talk above the sound of them. If you hung a sweaty shirt up outside, the 'hoppers would eat the collar off before you could get back to it. When they flew, they turned a blue day black.

So much happened and so much went wrong in those early days you wonder how the people hung on, and why they did. All the girls left. One of the boys was killed in the war—that was Ben. Another developed diabetes, couldn't ride, and had to go make a living at something else—that would be Alexander. Leo, Jerome, and Dan stayed on. Dan married his wife Mary, the schoolteacher, at Calypso in 1945. By that time they were running something like 7,000 steers. Mary was a homesteader's daughter.

When Dan and Mary married, the ranch had its own schoolhouse, an old railroad building brought across the river on the ice. But in 1965 they built a tram across the Yellowstone so the kids could catch the bus into Terry. That was the tram I saw upriver. They called it the Flying Susan. At one time twenty children rode the Flying Susan. Now there are none, but they still use it to cross back and forth.

Dan and Mary had nine children. Of the six girls,

only one married a cowboy. She was in the hospital now having nearly severed her hand in the flywheel of a feed grinder. The doctors had sewed it back on but weren't sure how much she'd be able to use it.

"You're lucky," Dan says, "could be flow ice this time of the year." He's seen the Yellowstone freeze over by mid-November. One fall he'd crossed two hundred head of cattle on the ice. A hell of a mess when they'd spooked and started running, milling around out on that ice. In the spring he can hear the ice moving from the house, great big cakes as big as a house, popping up into the air, falling off into the river, booming at night like cannon shot. Sometimes the cakes stack up and make jams, and the river backs up and floods. When that happens they wake up with the river in their front yard. "River don't flood as bad as it used to, now that all those creeks feeding it are dammed."

Ice broke the tram cable once, and the splice they made to fix it gives the car a jolt halfway across. A snag caught the cable one spring as the hired man and his family were crossing, and everyone on shore held their breath as the tree played the cable like a fiddle bow and then shot off downstream.

"Well," he says, "Mary'll be worried. Best be going. You better come to the house and have some lunch."

But I say if he doesn't mind I'd just as soon stay. He doesn't.

As we've talked, the storm's blown itself out. Stark yellow plains light knifes through the clouds, touching the badlands past the Powder River's mouth. There's a warm wind blowing.

"Chinook," Dan says.

"I've lucked out again."

"Don't humor yourself," he says, stomping off to his pickup, "winter's a' comin'." The little American flag on his aerial flaps itself into a blur as he drives away.

The chinook blows all night. The drifts against the dugout melt. A leak drips from the roof and turns the floor to mud. Time to move along.

Out on the river, tumbleweeds run off the flat gumbo banks into the water like lemmings, bounce across the channel, and roll across the prairie—nothing to stop them in a hundred miles.

A roar of rapids. What's this?

Yellow-Bear, according to Clark, named because a grizzly was standing out in the river on the rocks when they passed. The corps shot at it, as they'd done at most bears since they'd left St. Louis. But instead of dying or retreating, the grizzly plunged into the water and swam after them.

The wind blows the wave crests into silver manes, river dropping through red lance points of rock. For the first time in a long time I scramble to get the boat in order, throwing loose things into the ammo cans at my feet, strapping down the tent, bedding, and coats. Remembering all the gold-laden Mackinaws that sank here, all the steamers, and the dreary scene upriver, I kick the hip boots off, and put the life jacket on. I've been using it as a cushion. Stand to look it over. Clark says there's one runnable channel on the left—one blue tongue through the bear's mouth. We skim down it with hardly a stroke, rising and falling through the tail waves without a splash.

I pass Yorks Dry River, named by Clark for his black slave.

"The object which appeared to astonish the Indians most was Captain Clark's servant York," Merriwether Lewis wrote on October 9, 1805, "a remarkably stout, strong negro. They had never seen a being of that color, and therefore flocked around him to examine the extraordinary monster. By way of amusement he told them that he had once been a wild animal, caught and tamed by his master; and to convince them showed them feats of strength which, added to his looks, made him more terrible than we wished him to be."

Few of the Indians had seen a white man, much less a black. Fascinated, the men smoked and joked and tried to rub his color off. That first cold winter the expedition spent on the Missouri among the Mandans was remembered by the people as the Winter the Blackman Froze His Man Part.

All of which made it easier for Edward Rose, the mulatto outlaw and former pirate, to move among the people when he came up the Yellowstone with Manuel Lisa in 1807.

"A dogged, sullen, silent fellow," as described by Washington Irving, "with a sinister aspect and more of the savage than the civilized man in his appearance."

When Lisa sent Colter out to drum up trade among the Crow, he also sent out Rose. But Rose promptly gave away all his presents to a nearby village and stayed for the rest of his life, coming out now and then to guide or interpret or deliver a message. He told Ashley to watch out for his hair in 1823 at the Arikara villages. Zeonias Leonard saw him at war with his adopted people against the Blackfeet in 1832.

The Blackfeet had fortified themselves on a hill where they withstood several ineffectual Crow charges. "Finally the old negro," as Leonard called Rose, "came to their aid. He upbraided them for their failure, exhorted them to show more spirit . . . told them that if the red man was afraid to go amongst his enemy, he would show them that a black man was not, and he lept from the rock on which he had been standing, and, looking neither to the right nor to the left, made for the fort as fast as he could run. The Indians guessing his purpose, and inspired by his words and fearless example, followed close to his heels, and were in the fort dealing destruction to the right and left nearly as soon as the old man."

Rose died by touching a spark to a powder keg, preferring suicide to the inventive torture planned by the Arikara who'd finally caught him outside Fort Cass at the Bighorn's mouth.

James Beckwith, the third of this black trio, came up with Ashley and "thereafter entered upon a series of experiences that filled every month of his life with more adventures than the average mountaineer could boast of in twice as many years."

While he was running a tavern in California in 1851,

Beckwith related his experiences to Thomas Bonner, a newspaper man with a flair for imagination. "Both worthies were fond of rum," a detractor stated, "and the more they drank the more Indians Beckwith would recall having slain, his eloquence increasing in inverse ratio to the diminishing rum supply, and at last he would slap the 'squire' on the knee and chortle, 'Paint her up, Bonner! Paint her up!'"

Beckwith, too, found life with the Crow attractive, and the people loved him, perhaps because he was such a braggart. In 1868 Beckwith lead a colonel Carrington through the land of the Sioux. While visiting his Crow friends, trying to learn of Red Cloud's whereabouts, Beckwith died. Some say poisoned—the Crow didn't want him to leave, he brought them luck—and some say an accident. And some say he'd just finally wore out. Last of the mountain men.

At Powder River's mouth I row over for a look: red water into brown, the Yellowstone's last great artery— a mile wide and an inch deep. "Powder River let 'er buck!" cowboys used to cry. Water from the parched Wyoming hills three hundred miles south, water from all of Montana east of the Tongue and south of the mainstem, water from Jakes Creek, Bay Horse, Baking Powder, Broadus, and the Little Powder, from Slaughter Creek, Big Teepee, Swede, Ash, and Mizpah. To name a few.

If industry had its way with the Powder, not a drop would reach the Yellowstone.

The wind's so strong we're blown ashore and held against my will. It takes sweating and cursing and pulling at the oars to get us back midriver. Small wonder the steamer *Osceola* was blown to bits in a gale here in 1877.

"It was a fearful, fearful storm," the captain wrote his commodore in St. Louis. "We were caught in an open prairie country miles from timber and the storm came down upon us like an avenging fiend."

Clark called the Powder the Redstone, camped a mile down beneath a "spreading cottonwood tree," and spent the night worrying if buffalo were going to smash the boats.

No buffalo now, though I keep my eyes peeled for a skull. Four wind-crooked cottonwoods grow from the old one's seed, black and leafless against the blue sky. The only trees I've passed in miles, the only trees in sight.

A mile further and I stop, beach the boat, and walk ashore to visit the grave of Private William H. George, Company E, Seventh Cavalry, who died of wounds received on Reno Hill, June 26, 1876, and was buried at 4:00 A.M., July 3, while being sped back to Fort Lincoln on the *Far West*.

By 1883 there were 600,000 cattle in Montana Territory. The roundup that fall saw 27 camp wagons, 400 cowboys, and 4,000 horses encamped at the mouth of Crazy Woman Creek.

But in 1885 the drought began. The summer of 1885 was hot, the grass was sparse and cropped short. The summer of 1886 brought more of the same. That November it snowed, then thawed, and then froze again, forming a hard crust not even elk could break. The storms began on Christmas Eve and didn't stop for sixty days. It got colder than it'd ever been within memory. One cowboy said he wore two pairs of wool socks, Dutch woolens that came to his knees, moccasins, overshoes, two suits of heavy long underwear, overalls, chaps, a heavy shirt, wool gloves, mittens, a blanket-lined coat, a sealskin cap, and "in that way kept warm. But not any too warm."

The cattle drifted with the storm, floundered in coulees, walked off badland cliffs, piled up in the river bottoms, and broke the ice. Spring was ripe with death. Sixty percent of Montana's cattle had died.

Out of work cowboys turned to rustling, leading four years later to the Johnson County War down Buffalo, Wyoming, way. The Wyoming Cattleman's Association hired a trainload of Texas assassins to eliminate the undesirables—which included homesteaders and sheepmen as well as rustlers. But it was the end of the line for the hard men no matter how the cattlemen cut the deck. Fences and farmers were here to stay.

Last spring I drove down to the Padlock Ranch, which holds rangeland from the Yellowstone south to the head of the Tongue and still runs roundup wagons and conducts roundups in turn-of-the-century fashion. I rode out to the wagon with the range detective, George Cunningham, bouncing along over the sagebrush of the Crow Indian Reservation through a pair of ruts, a dust plume rising behind us. Sage hens flushed, chuckling off from where they'd been dusting, and George's dog Mike went crazy barking each time. George had been a detective for the Padlock for twenty years. Stealing was quite a problem. A lot of people were poaching beef. He traveled some 250,000 acres in his pickup, watching over some 10,000 cows.

He said the outfit had a new cook this spring. Wagon cooks were getting scarce. The old guys didn't want the hard life anymore. Once the outfit had a cook who wore a white chef's hat and made things those cowboys had never heard of, much less eaten. When the roundup was over, the fellow left and was never heard from again; he went to Paris or someplace like that. Then they had another fellow who spit on the griddle to check its temperature. Even made the old cowboys grimace. A good cook was the heart of a range outfit. The pay was so bad and the work so hard that the cooking had to be good or none of the cowboys would stay.

It was sunset when we found the wagon down along Tullock Creek, an island of canvas amid a sea of sage and grass-covered hills. A fat, sweating man with a moustache and black hair came out of the cooktent, wiping his floury hands on an apron.

"You lost?"

His name was Jim. He'd been traveling through the country when his car broke down in Sheridan. He'd heard the Padlock was looking for a cook and applied.

They asked if he could cook and he'd said he thought he could. "So here I am."

He was from Oregon, and the hardest part of the job was not having trees and mountains around. And he didn't like the heat. Cowboys were entirely different from anybody he'd ever worked with. They seemed to like the isolation. He didn't. He liked to read and he liked music. Around cowboys if you didn't play cards there was nothing to do at night. "All them guys have already gone to bed." He couldn't get enough books. "I don't know if I'll make it six more weeks."

Floyd Workman, the wagon boss, had the darkest tanned face and hands I've ever seen. He'd worked cows all of his fifty years. His arms were white above the cuffs of his pinstriped Western shirt and his forehead was white above his hat line. He sat on an upside-down milkcan in the canvas cooktent, rolling cigarettes and smoking, answering my questions. He was twenty years older than the oldest hand, and forty years older than the youngest, who was twelve. He said there weren't many cowboys left. Cowboys could make better money working in the mines, driving a truck, most anything else. A man had to be dedicated to work as hard as cowboys worked for a hundred dollars a week and grub, sleeping on the ground. Mostly they got kids looking for a way to spend the summer. A few rounders. Not much call these days for a man who just wanted to ride. Cowboy today's got to be a jack-of-all-trades: drive a pickup, fix fence, doctor cattle, grease windmills.

Spring roundup lasts from Memorial Day until the Fourth of July here on the northern place. They'd be branding down on the southern end until August. Unless a man got fired, he stayed with the wagon for the duration. No trips, no alcohol, no vehicles. Each man is issued six horses. The riding begins at dawn, gathering cattle and driving them into portable corrals. They branded about three hundred head a day. There wasn't anything romantic about working for the wagon. The wagon was a tool—they used it because the Padlock's pastures were larger than most ranches; if they drove back and forth from home, all their time would be spent on the road. Pickups couldn't move in that country when it rained. Someday the ranch owners would figure out something different and wouldn't have to use the wagon anymore. "The good old days were the hard old days."

I woke to Floyd's "Whoooeeeee!" at four the next morning and made my way slowly toward the cooktent in the darkness. Spurs jingled in the grass. A half-dozen cowboys were already in the tent, hats silhouetted by lantern light on the canvas. Coyotes were howling, and a curlew made a curious, quavering high-pitched bupbupbupbupbup sound overhead. A full moon was setting. The stars were still out.

Inside, the men sat cross-legged and bleary-eyed in the dirt, heads bowed, silent, coats buttoned to scarfed throats, drinking coffee. A can of Bugler tobacco was making the rounds, the day's first smokes were being rolled.

A young boy was sitting on a metal folding chair in the corner, knees shaking. Though he tried to hide it, his tin plate vibrated against his fork.

"Hell, don't worry kid," said Butch, a Nevada buckaroo in a white shirt, black vest, and red scarf, "that ol' Roany hoss's only killed a few men."

Jim set out trays of gravy, scrambled eggs, and biscuits. He'd been cooking since three.

The two wranglers ate first, already wearing their chaps and spurs, then left, saddled up their horses, and rode off. Everyone else took their time with a last cup of coffee and smoke and then wandered out to the rope corral where their saddles lay covered by yellow slickers on the ground.

We could hear the wranglers whooping and whistling and then the horses running, hooves striking the earth like a coming storm. They poured down off the hillside, manes and tails glowing in the sun's rise, legs swishing through high creek-bottom grass, funneled into the corral through a ten-foot opening, blowing and snorting and squealing. Ropers moved among the milling horses inside, shaking loops out of coils in their hands, sending them hissing into the herd, delicately turning and sliding over horses' heads onto necks.

It was moving day, and the camp was struck and packed within an hour, bed and mess wagons rumbling and jangling, wheels creaking in the rutted road, followed by the remuda, nudged along by hollering riders—the whole procession one loud, dusty roar, passing from my view, leaving only the sound of red-winged blackbirds in the marsh grass down along Tullock Creek and the wind passing over the buffalo grass beneath the big sky.

I float into evening among scoria bluffs: strange, crazy shapes rising several hundred feet from the river's edge, striped black, vermilion, ochre, and gray. As bleak as they are beautiful. Camp is up a coulee; no side channels here, no islands. No driftwood. Mud up to my knees. I spread the sleeping bag in needle grass beneath sagebrush, being careful of the prickly pear.

Greasewood fire shadows dance on yellow gumbo walls. Coyotes howl. The wind whines and whimpers in cracks and crevices. Bits of eroding cliff trickle into the river. Bats dart among the stars. Badlands.

For the first time on the trip I can't sleep. Stryder moves about restlessly, looking off. There're no grizzlies here, I think. The last wolf (were I afraid of wolves) was killed for bounty in 1926. No Sioux out there. No road or town within miles. All the rattlesnakes denned. No irate coyote trappers. We hope. Something nameless then.

I move closer to the boat and fall asleep as soon as my head touches the life jacket pillow.

During the night I wake to Stryder leaving. Not again, I think, calling him back. But later he moves off anyway, following his nose to something in the wind. He barks several times, then quits.

Just before dawn, clouds boil in, turning the sunrise into storm light; the clouds are pink-bottomed, then blue, then black with a half moon showing through.

The badlands are bathed in yellow light: the reds, blacks, whites, and yellows reflected as a rainbow in the river.

The current's slow. I row for an hour to warm up, then drift.

Past Sheridan Butte, Crooked Creek, Sullivan, Lost Boy, and Arndt—plugged with car bodies. At the Terry Bridge, I moor the boat, tie Stryder up, and walk into town. No excuse. I just need to look around.

When I think of the Yellowstone, when I try and remember when I first heard its name, I see it as it is here, flowing wide and sluggishly beneath the Terry Bridge—but I see a different bridge, older and narrower, clattering as I crossed it in the pickup with my uncle, Cleon Lesh. It was late May and snowing. A raw spring wind whined through a crack in the window. A bloating cow body turned over and over in the current. I was fresh from the city in my wheat jeans and penny loafers, on my way to a summer job. 1966.

My Grandad Lesh had been a cowboy in the 1900s, working for the Seven Wagon outfit in southern Wyoming and northern Colorado. He had shot out streetlights in the town of Greeley with the pistol I carry now, and had terrorized schoolgirls on the sidewalks—my grandmother had been one. He had ridden broncs for breakfast and had roped wild horned cattle. And then he had laid his saddle down, swapped his Levi's for overalls, his Cheyenne-made boots for homesteader's lace-ups. Of the ten kids he and grandmother raised, only my Uncle Cleon got the reins to Grandad's wild cowboy genes. At fourteen he ran away to a Wyoming ranch; he wintered for a few years in a line camp breaking colts for spare change. "That Clen can ride anything," Grandad used to say.

After a Navy stint, he married the church organist, Lonetta Clary, and tried to settle down on a dryland farm. But corn didn't fit his hand nor irrigation boots his soul. He sold out, moved to Montana, and bought a ranch north of Bad Route Creek.

I still see him as I did that first day, with a three-day growth of whiskers, black silk scarf about his throat, calf-blood and tractor-grease-stained sowbelly Stetson with a narrow, turned-down brim on his head. He stood nearly seven feet tall in his high-heeled riding boots, his yellow slicker spattered with mud, in the center of a muddy corral, holding a snorting colt by a halter with one large hand. "Here's your horse, boy. Don't spoil him."

That first morning I learned how to read a brand (top to bottom, inside out, left to right), to start a well pump, and to drive a tractor. I spent the summer cutting, raking, baling, and stacking hay. I never did learn to ride. The colt always came home alone. I turned more cows through fences than I put back in the herd, broke machinery, stuck pickups. But it was the greatest summer of my life, and the next I came back for more.

Joe Roos ranched west of my uncle's place. He wore pop-bottle-thick glasses, flatland shoes, overalls, and was the truest cowman my uncle knew. Joe was afraid of heights and worked a deal with my uncle to oil his windmills. And then at the Terry Fair we saw Joe up in the Ferris wheel, laughing and throwing popcorn. The next day, as we were driving by Joe's place, we spotted him out on his windmill. "If I can ride one of those things," he told my uncle, "I guess I can climb my own mill."

Nels Undem's place was to the south. Nels lost his feet in a blizzard, and the doctors in Miles City said he'd never walk again. But Nels bet them double or nothing on his bill and stumped around in cowboy boots for the rest of his life, swinging himself aboard his horse with powerful arms. Nels's cattle saw people twice a year; and he let them keep their horns. His corrals were made of railroad ties. In the spring the men glassed for the herds from hilltops, raced to get around them in pickups, then jumped saddled horses out of the back and tried to head them home. Nels's hired man, Arnie, lived in a log dugout with a sod roof on which he'd piled all the buffalo skulls he'd found. During the summer, grass and flowers grew on the roof. He said he'd come across a wintering den of rattlesnakes in the badlands once, steam rising from a crack in the ground like a coal seam burning underground.

Downtown Terry hasn't changed. One wide, windy, dusty street and a dozen two-story buildings: post office, bank, store, hotel, and hardware store. At Young's Bar and Cafe I order breakfast, the first I haven't cooked for a while. The pickups come rolling in about eight. Men with short-cropped hair drink coffee sitting on stools, get up and walk around the counter to pour their own refills. They eat farm eggs with deep yellow

yolks, sunny-side up, with white triangle slices of but-
tered toast and side orders of bacon and hashbrowns.
They wear ball caps with logos advertising Cenex and
John Deere and Caterpillar across the front. Some are
in coveralls but most are in Levi's and cowboy boots,
Western shirts with pearl snaps. While Roy Young does
the short orders, his wife Vera does the waitressing.
Down in the bar end, surrounded by a collection of Jim
Beam decanters and C. M. Russell prints, the early
morning hardcore roll the dice for a first drink.

"How the hell old are you, Jim?" asks a man next to
me of an obvious old-timer in a cowboy hat. Old Jim,
who really does look the part and's been playing this
game every morning for ages, says, "When I came here
that red bluff was a hole in the ground."

"Say, Jim, I hear your wife left you," someone says.
Old Jim pours his coffee into a saucer, takes a sip.

"Yahhh. Old lady wanted indoor plumbin'." Everyone chuckles. All the rest of the talk is of oil and how
much they want it to come.

"I hear that up in Sydney those oil lease fellas start
lining their briefcases up on the courthouse steps before
light and then go drink a cup of coffee and wait for the
place to open up."

My uncle once told me that to make it ranching, you
either had to own the land or the cattle. He owed for
both, and after two years of disparity and nineteen-cent
calves he had to give the Bad Route place up. Now he
manages a big outfit on Pumpkin Creek.

Nels Undem died of a heart attack. Arnie Tunum

went on a bender and never came home. The Smallis boys are married, the Mydinger girls as well. Joe Roos turned his place over to Joe Junior, moved to town, and became a janitor at the school. So and so's kid came back from the war all screwed up; lived in a cave out on his dad's place. The Indian kid who was bit by a rattle-snake was mistaken for a North Vietnamese and blown away by his own troops. All the ranch daughters have run away to become anything but ranchers' wives. A lot of the country's fenced that wasn't ten years ago, a lot of prairie's been turned into winter wheat.

Past Ash Creek, Cedar, Coal, O'Fallon, Pine, and Cot-tonwood. I've gone all afternoon without a coat, bask-ing in the sunshine. No wind. Geese and ducks flush. Sandhill cranes mill overhead. Magpies and jays give me hell from the banks. Cows bawl for their departed calves—it's shipping time. Cattle trucks rumble across dirt roads.

The river's straight and slow, a big lake. Maybe a half mile wide. I don't touch an oar all afternoon unless I ab-solutely have to, just spin along.

Past Plum Coulee—no plums there anymore. Past Hatchet and Bad Route Creek, Dry, and Crackerbox.

At sunset the water glows like coals.

I beach in twilight, pulling the boat onto shore. Overhead a line of cranes floats by on set wings, ptero-dactyl shapes swirling, an outlandish chorus of squeaks and rasps, whistles and shrieks, croaks and rattles. There are hundreds of birds circling, gliding lower and

lower. I sit still and press the dog flat, lower my face,
watch from the corner of my eyes. A thousand cranes.
Three thousand—a storm cloud of cranes, wings like a
wind, a rain of white craneshit spattering the beach,
birds dropping like falling leaves.

But at last I have to raise my head. The incoming
birds flare, startling the settling ranks into a frightened,
clattering takeoff. Within seconds we're alone on the
beach listening to water lap past shore, the crane voices
fading upriver into the night.

It's a gray, bleak morning. The wind's raising two-foot
swells, blowing dust devils across the flats. I start the
day with a curse, putting my back and all my strength
into each stroke, pulling and grunting, grunting and
pulling, looking over my shoulder every ten strokes to
make sure of where I'm going. Let up and I'm blown
two raft lengths upriver.

"My situation a very disagreeable one," Clark wrote
while passing through this vicinity, "in an open canoe
without the possibility of keeping myself dry. The
country through which we passed is in every respect
like that passed through yesterday . . . at 2 P.M. I was
obliged to land to let the buffalow cross over . . . it took
them four hours to cross."

At 2:00 P.M. (my guess, I carry no watch), I pass
through the town of Glendive. A three-bridge town,
traffic roaring. A horror of metal and pipes and wires
and jagged chunks of concrete riprap. I'm not even
tempted to stop. Beneath a bridge on a spit of sand, two

fishermen, in white painters' clothes, fish for pike—so they say—spotted painters' caps on their heads, both sitting on paint cans.

In the afternoon I make a remarkable discovery. By reading the pattern of the wind on the water I can make my way through. So simple and yet so magnificent I laugh out loud. Ho. Ho. Ho. Like Santa Claus.

Sail past Cotton Creek, Deer, Threemile, Sevenmile, Morgan, and Thirteenmile.

Badlands and plains give way to cottonwood bottoms. The river grows more sluggish by the mile, twisting through wide meanders, shattering into a half-dozen different channels, bending a little more northeast, tugging me steadily toward the Dakotas.

In the evening the wind drops and the river becomes still. Cottonwoods on either side of me for the first time in several days—I feel as if I'm among friends. I put a coat on to keep the chill off, tuck the oar handles beneath my knees, and sit drifting, enjoying the peace, letting the long plains spaces fill the emptiness between thoughts.

I camp on the first big island in sixty miles. There's a white sand beach, and all the stones are moss covered, bleached. It takes 150 feet of rope to moor the boat to a snag on shore. Mud sucks at my boots as I haul gear into the trees. Stryder romps with a stick, running and growling, bucking into the air, begging for a wrestle or a toss, something to swim for.

I light the lantern and gather wood. Then dig a shallow pit in the sand, and encircle it with agate boulders big as footballs. I make a rice stew for the main course. An apple for dessert. When the dishes are done—scrubbed in sand, river rinsed—I place a metal washtub on the rocks and build a bonfire to boil drinking water. I inflate the air mattress, strip, and climb into the bag—safe, warm, and done for another day. Propped on an elbow, I watch the flames burn into embers.

Often at night I wake to a noise. Twig snap. Coyote howl. Chugapopping of an oil well way off. Stryder walking around. I lie and watch the stars, contemplating the infinite, the milky stardust desert. An occasional comet streak or meteor shower. The red bleeping of a satellite or plane.

A clear dawn. I cook a leisurely breakfast while squatting in the sun and drinking coffee. Load the boat and then take a walk through the cottonwoods to the island's north end. Spend another hour studying deer, crane, and coon tracks, picking up stones that strike my fancy, throwing sticks for Stryder.

The day turns hot, burning me out of clothes all the way down to Levi's and T-shirt. How long can this last? Not long. I begin bundling back up as soon as the sun slips across noon.

When I hear the Intake Dam and see its telltale gouts of foam, my first angry thought is to run it. But standing up and taking a look ends that foolishness.

After the drought in the 1930s, people thought a lot more about water. Farmers were moving into the Yel-

lowstone Valley and turning the sod into wheat, the
gamma grass into corn. They tamed the wild cattle
bergs into towns—the kids needed schools and teachers, places to buy shoes, Sunday school. The government laid claim to most of the land so recently vacated
of Indians and buffalo, leased it back to ranchers, gave
it to homesteaders—anything to make it produce and
save it from "going to waste."

The first farmer wave starved and froze and dried
out, but the second and third clung. They saw water
running downriver, an infinite source, so they dammed
the creeks into ponds, tapped the aquifer with pipes,
and sucked hungrily at the river with pumps. "All hell
needs is water," they said, and the prairie bloomed.

Now and then the farmers formed themselves into
irrigation districts and pooled their money to invest in
pumping stations, in canals and diversions. Intake Dam
was such a diversion. New and improved tractors had
made large-scale farming possible, and large farms re-
quire large amounts of water.

It was a sad time for rivers. Up on the Missouri, the
Bureau of Reclamation (reclaiming water from the sea)
and the Army Corps of Engineers ("Keep Busy!") were
building Fort Peck. Down south, they were attacking
the Colorado. In the east, the Tennessee Valley Authority was flooding the Appalachians. The backs of the
Sierra rivers were being broken. In salmon country, the
salmon were dying in stagnant Columbia pools.

Somehow the Yellowstone has been overlooked, the
last living reminder of how all rivers once flowed.

Meanwhile our wants, fantasies, and population increase.

Intake drops water six feet over a ledge. There's no channel around. On its other side, fishermen cast into the foam from lawn chairs, cool beers resting in the sand. A dozen men, a few women, none of whom will ever see sixty again. All watch me carry my junk overland, no one saying a thing, while Stryder frisks with an Irish setter.

Finally a man follows me over to see the boat.

"Heck," he says, "you should of said something. I got a pickup." Which he brings, and I load, completing the portage in two trips. I give him a dead goose. He thanks me, holding it around the neck at arm's length, and nothing more is said. He goes back to fishing and I to pumping and loading.

"What do you catch here?" I ask the owner of the setter.

"Skipjack," he says.

That's all.

What Intake is famous for are paddlefish, a prehistoric cross between gar and swordfish with a long, blunt, fleshy snout and blind-pig eyes, bluish gray, anywhere from fifteen to sixty pounds, two to ten feet in length. Paddlefish live in the Missouri and run up the Yellowstone to spawn in April. That's all anyone knows about them. Not where they go, what they do, or when they run back down. Paddlefish don't have much of a mouth, they strain microscopic life through their teeth.

The only way to catch them is by casting a treble hook from the bank, reeling it back through the spawners milling around in the water below Intake Dam, and hauling the unfortunate fish ashore with brute strength and hundred-pound test line.

There's just enough water going over Intake Dam to let a paddlefish swim up the Yellowstone to spawn. Take away a few more inches and the paddlefish wouldn't survive. That thin fact has helped the Montana Department of Fish, Wildlife, and Parks hold water users at bay.

There are folks who say the paddlefish should go the way of the buffalo. "You can't hold up progress for a fish most people've never heard of." They'd leave the nesting geese high and dry as well, suck the river dry for energy. On an economic scale, free rivers are hard to justify.

As the evening chill comes on, the fishermen leave. Done with the boat, cleaned and patched, I drag it out into the current and climb aboard, row downriver a mile and camp on a gravel bar in the dark. Eat a cold supper sitting on the boat, studying maps by lantern light.

A big rain comes up about midnight, and for the first time in a month I put up the tent.

At Crane I go ashore to mail film. The postmaster says I'm lucky. There could be flow ice this time of year. I say I know.

From the counter's other side he takes my last few

dollars for a deer tag. Stryder holds the town pack at
bay outside the door.

It takes half a dozen rocks to see us back to the boat.
Suspicious people stare at me from finger-parted curtains, snapping them closed if I stare back.

I can feel winter's raw edge this morning. There's ice
at the river's edge. All the leaves are gone. The sky is
empty of geese. A bright sun gives no warmth. I wear
my overcoat, mittens, and insulated pacs, and only lift
the wool flaps of my cap when I need to hear.

The river's wide and brown, parting around cottonwood islands measured in square miles. Occasional
bluffs. I spin slowly down one channel or another, staying close to the banks, just out of sweeper reach, one eye
out for snags, the other watching for deer.

Past Box Elder Creek, Linden, War Dance, Cottonwood, Dry, Burns, Beef Slough, Smith, Dunlop, Shad-
well, Sears, and Crane.

Past the gumbo maze of Devil's Canyon which I've
no time to explore, past Graveyard and Garden Coulee,
Mary's Island, Elk, and Seven Sisters.

Finally, knowing I'm going too fast, knowing how
soon it's all going to be over, I stop on a nameless island
to hunt.

The wind has as much to do with the island's selec-
tion as any other reason, coming up suddenly, spitting
snow, making my arms hurt, driving me to a beach, and
pinning the boat against shore.

The gravel and sand along the beach are covered
with deer tracks: running tracks, big bucks sunk up

to their hocks. The doe and fawn tracks are so light they're like feathered impressions, barely there at all. So many tracks it looks as if a band of sheep moved through. Near the willow and grass, the tracks funnel into trails, headed for the cottonwood/rosebush interior.

I follow a step at a time, Stryder behind, sniffing, stopping when I stop, scent so fresh I can hear him sucking it in out of the grass and off of the trees. I push my way through young cottonwoods, pencil straight, thick as quills, to an open wash of sand and grass, an old channel. The deer paths cross and go down it. I no more than leave the trees and start down the channel when I flush two deer, hear them crashing through the brush on the left and turn in time to see two white rumps arcing into gray brush. Walk up the channel and see a dozen more: two small bucks, the rest does and last year's fawns, all gray as cottonwoods, sleek and well fed. Sometimes I see them just as they jump to their feet—a flicker of movement, a deer materializing where there was no deer before, then gone—sometimes jumping straight across the wash in front of me, one, two, three, two more, always at just enough interval I'm never ready, far enough away I can't risk a shot.

The wash turns to rosebushes and I cut west toward the tallest cottonwoods I can see. Difficult walking. Too many leaves. Twice I hear things moving off, stop but see nothing. Thorns snag my overcoat and scratch my hands, scar the gunstock. I wade through some brush, holding the rifle over my head. In other places I have to

forge a new route. Here and there I find where a buck
has rubbed bark from a tree with antlers. There are
small patches of torn-up earth, and deer pellets underfoot.

By late afternoon I've worked my way around the island back to the boat. The sun's out. I pitch the tent on
sand in the brush, gather firewood, lead the boat to a
secluded cove, and set off up the island's other side.

It's more of the same. Deer stream away through
thick brush, their white rears like bouncing balls. I let
myself become as much like a deer as I can—let their
tracks and trails take me to deer places: the lush grass
meadows, the thickets where rosehips linger, the small
pools of water. There are warm deer-beds in the grass
beneath a cottonwood so large around that hugging it I
can't touch fingertips.

Returning to camp in the twilight I find a buffalo
skull half buried in dirt, dig it out with my knife and
carry it back to contemplate, by firelight, after supper.

What've you seen old bull, I wonder, feeling the
roughness of the horns, the cracks and splinters of a
century's erosion, the freeze and thaw of how many
winters. Were the cottonwoods young when you
crossed this island? What did you see through those
eyes? Did you die peacefully alone, wandered away
from the herd to starve, or did you succumb to wolves
and winter? Were you chased by horseback hunters?
Did one of Clark's men kill you with a musket? Were
you washed down in a flood? Stripped of your robe? Or
were your bones already turning to dust before your

nostrils ever stank of man, an endless sea of grass out your eyes, breeding cows, siring calves, butting heads, nothing but wind and wolf howls, sighs, grunts, and bellows of the herd. Flames from my fire now dance in your empty sockets, hands from a different world disturb your rest, searching your old bones for clues.

Dawn. Frosted grass. Ghostly fingers of mist float among the cottonwoods. I creep out of the tent and into the woods, footfalls cushioned by dampness, cold gunmetal in my hands. A goose honks out on a sandbar at the island's tip.

I take one step at a time, stand still, search with my eyes. At the edge of the wash I sit with my back against a tree, Stryder lying reluctantly beside me, head flattened to the ground. One hand's on the gun, the other scratching the dog's ears. A coyote howls. Just once. A gun booms, way off.

I sit until my fingers and toes are numb with cold. A breeze drops the frost off the leaves like rain. Nothing. I straighten out my legs, let Stryder stretch, light my pipe. Stand. In front of me a gray doe walks forward out of gray shadow, fifty yards away, reaching out to pluck a rosehip; a young buck follows behind, forked horns polished brown. I tap Stryder on the nose and he goes down. Deer eyes on me, deer frozen midstep, forelegs lifted. I raise the rifle and settle the sights over the doe's back to the buck's head, pull the hammer back. Click. Click. Wood cold against my cheek. Squeeze. Flame and thunder. The gun leaps as if alive, punches my shoulder. The buck sags slowly backward to the ground.

"Move on," I say to the doe, still staring at me as I lower the gun; but she doesn't leave until I step forward, and even then she walks.

I prop the gun against a tree and squat beside the buck in the bloody grass; an eye, watching me, turns dull. One moment I'm filled with sadness, and the next I'm reaching for my knife. I roll him onto his back and cut up to the brisket through his steaming chest.

Deer heart and liver for breakfast, ribs for lunch, backstrap for supper. A day of feasting beside the fire, of lazy contemplation watching the river pass.

Rain turns to snow during the night. I wake to gray storm clouds breaking and shove into the current. Two whitetail bucks plunge off the mainland and into the river, swimming across in front of me, ten yards off the bow, eyes wild, snorting, heads just above the surface. They strike shore running.

"The river is now a mile wide," wrote Clark, "less rapid and more divided by islands and bars of sand and mud than hitherto; the low grounds too are more extensive, and contain a greater quantity of cottonwood, ash, and willow trees. On the northwest is a low, level plain; on the southeast are some rugged hills, on which we saw, without being able to approach, some bighorns. The buffalo and elk, as well as the pursuers of both, the wolves, are in great numbers. . . . The bears, which gave so much trouble on the head of the Missouri, are equally fierce in this quarter. This morning one of them, which was on a sand-bar as the boat passed, raised himself on his hind feet; and after looking at us, plunged in and swam at us. He was received with three balls in the body; he then turned round and made for the shore. . . . The boats escaped with difficulty between two herds of buffalo which were crossing the river."

At noon I pass through Sidney. There's smoke and generator hum from a candy-striped Montana Power smokestack. There's a sickly sweet smell of sugar beets from a sugar beet factory. Traffic roars across a bridge—shift change. Crushed car bodies line the shore. Out of town, the river's banks are 'dozed flat down to the water's edge. The streams coming in are polluted with oil. There's the smell of oil, oil rigs pumping, fires of natural gas lighting the sky with pulsing auras. Nonstop machine roar. Seismic blasting.

No matter how hard I row, there's no escape, no relief. I camp on a mudflat beneath a power tower, lines humming overhead. There's a trailerhouse a hundred yards away with a drilling platform rearing next to it, the derrick shining like a missile in the white light of a hundred halogens. Engines hum and slam. Pipes bang. Steam and smoke.

After supper I walk to the trailerhouse and knock. "Yeah?" says a voice. I open the door. An acne-scarred guy sits with his black, pointed-toe cowboy boots on a desk. He's cleaning a pistol.

"Mind if I look around?" Me.

"What for?" Him.

"Just interested in the oil."

"You're in luck, we're pulling the pipe for a test. Soon's the geologist comes, he'll tell you everything you wanna' know."

He's the pusher. His job is to live with the rig all the time, making sure everything's running.

"Well, you've got a nice view," I say.

"You think so, huh? I guess I been in the country too long." He was interested in hunting. "This weather, everything's laying low."

I'd pictured the geologist, Herb Kane, in blue jeans and a down vest, as lean and spare and flinty and serious as the rocks he studies, but he's a short, jovial, round man in his sixties with an Arrow shirt and slacks, a walrus mustache, diamond rings, and a gold chain around his neck. He's not into rocks, he's into oil. Oil is all he knows. Oil's what he loves. Oil burns like a fever in him.

Herb Kane's first job was burying pipe for two-bits a chunk. He was an orphan kid. Later a roughneck, jug hustler, shooter, driller, and surveyor. He yells all of this at me in the trailerhouse, pouring cup after cup of coffee. At first I think he's angry, the way he yells, but it's only because the rigs have deafened him.

In 1943 a Jerry sniper put him in a wheelchair. The doctors said he'd never use his legs, but he went to school on the army's disablement money, studied geology, and whipped the paralysis. In 1951 when Ameranda—owned by H. L. Hunt—sent six company rigs into the Dakotas, Herb Kane was the supervisor. He was the first geologist to strike a producing well in the Williston Basin (in which this part of Montana is technically included), and he's worked on more producing wells than anyone since. He now works on retainer for a Houston company, is the supervising geologist on seven wells, and calls his territory southern Saskatchewan, southern Manitoba, eastern Montana, eastern Wyoming, and all the Dakotas. He puts 150,000 miles a year on his pickup. The company provides standing motel rooms in Williston, Dickinson, Billings, and Casper. He's on call twenty-four hours a day, seven days a week, and for this earns a grand a day.

"This country," he yells, "this whole half of the Yellowstone drainage sits atop the biggest coal pile in the world.

"Where there's coal there's oil!"

In 1972 there were only 9 rigs working in the whole Williston Basin. There's 150 now, more coming in, and more going down every day—2,300 wells have gone down in the last five years. Fourteen out of fifteen wells are dry holes. "It costs a million three to drill a dry hole!

"It's the biggest gamble in the world! I been in the oil business forty-two years, yet if somebody laid a million bucks on the table and said to invest it, damn if I'd put it into oil. The guy that'd hawk everything to drill the next rig. That's an oilman!

"Some of the landowners resist," he says, "but in the end they've little choice. If there's oil, it'll be found and gotten out. Only a matter of time. They're paid well for their trouble. We're paying some folks $200 an acre on a ten-year lease. Hey! Think of all the millions and millions of acres leased. The millions and millions of dollars involved."

Oil was the only way Herb had ever heard of for people to get something for nothing. "These ranchers are reaping the benefit of their forefathers, getting rich on land that takes twenty acres to feed a cow. Agriculture used to be the number-one industry in North Dakota. Now it's oil!"

He takes me on a tour of the rig, walking up a gangplank into the bowels, introducing me to the crew. The driller comes from Louisiana. "Generally," he says, "the crews are younger up here than they are down south, and the rigs up here are better to work on. For a windbreak down in Arkansas they use burlap."

The other four crewmen are from North Dakota, working in the tradition of their fathers who'd come in the 1950s when Ameranda opened the way.

"Sometimes," says the derrick hand, "it gets so fucking cold on top I come down with my beard iced."

The gas man, on hand for the test, says, "Sometimes H_2S rises out of a sour hole. One minute of gas and you have brain damage. Five minutes and you're gone."

"Down south," says the driller, "crews have shown up for work and found the crew before them all dead of gas."

"All this heavy metal," says the derrick hand, "you can get mangled in a second."

"Just a spark'll blow it up," says the pusher.

243

Herb's been through three oil field fires, been blown off a rig, lost a driller, and had five men down with gas. "But I'll tell you. This is one of the few businesses you can work yourself to the top from the bottom. This is America at its best!"

It takes all night to pull the pipe, all 12,000 feet of it, and make a test. No oil comes into the trap. Nor is there any sign.

The farmer who owns the land is on hand, a Norwegian, the original homesteader. He's still living in the same unpainted house with the same spare wife, and every piece of machinery he's ever owned is lined up neatly in front. The wife still carries water from the creek in a pail. "That new shopping mall in town," she says, "that came from oil money."

Afterward, in the trailerhouse office, Herb has sharp words with the driller. The test was conducted wrong. "You've blown about $15,000!"

"Well, I'm going to town," says the driller. His buddy from another rig is there to pick him up.

"Come on, man," the buddy yells, "it's my birthday and I ain't drunk yet."

"How old?" Herb asks.

"Nineteen," the buddy says.

Herb's going to Dickinson. His wife's flown up for the weekend. He'll be at a well near the confluence in a few days. I should catch up with him when I get off the river. "I will," I say, knowing I probably won't.

I try to sleep in, but can't. I get up and row hard, wanting to put the oil as far behind me as I can, to leave the sight of it, the smell, the noise, but it's not to be. All the long gray day I pass rig after rig, trailer courts, workmen in pickups eating lunch, bulldozers pushing over trees, the land flat and bleak and made a moonscape of.

In the afternoon snow comes and the temperature drops. I'm driven to shore, throw up the tent in a blizzard. No fire, no supper, asleep before dark.

The storm wails all night. I wake to the tent fly ripping its stakes out and snow crushing the tent's rear to the ground. Struggle into my heaviest winter clothes, eat a quick deer breakfast, and throw my gear into the raft, not caring that it's wet.

Snow blowing. Ice encases the oar blades. Black sky. Hunkering down low, I put my back into it, stern first, looking over a shoulder every hundred strokes.

Past Lone Tree Creek, Bennie, Deer, Horse, First and Second Hay, Charbonneau.

The last eight miles are the toughest of all, raft hanging on sandbars, blowing to a stop if I let up on the oars, snow blurring sight, stinging my face.

At twilight, the storm suddenly stops, as if swept aside by the Missouri, rushing in brown and big on my left. The raft, Stryder, and I glide quietly into the still lake formed by the two rivers' joining. I row the last few hundred yards to the muddy North Dakota shore in the dark.

In the morning I haul gear up on shore from the raft, piling it on the picnic grounds that overlook the confluence, and then walk up a dirt road to Fort Union. It's clear and cold, close to zero, snow squeaking underfoot.

Every now and then I hear geese or cranes and look up to watch them float high overhead. Specks. Three cars pass, swerving over to the road's other side to miss me; none stop and ask if I want a ride.

The fort used to be closer to the confluence but a flood in the 1930s shifted the channel and now it's three miles up the Missouri. Fort Union was once an imposing structure with blockhouses and palisades, buildings, and a massive gate to keep the Indians out. There's not much left now. Mounds of dirt from the Park Service's excavations. One building has been turned into a small museum and there are a few tipi skeletons left over from the living history program.

My friend Gerard works as the historian. He's there alone. It's Sunday. He comes out of the door and stands in his Park Service greens with a smile on his face.

"Echick," he says.

"Echick," I answer.

"I been lookin' for you every day, buddy," he says, giving me a great slap on the back. We go into the office and sit, drinking coffee, visiting, while Stryder runs around to all the windows and stands on his hind legs looking in.

Gerard gets off work at four. I say I'll wait around, look things over, maybe finish unloading the boat.

I walk out over the frozen ground where Kenneth McKensie walked and talked and drank Madeira wine with Maximilian and Karl Bodmer, past the remains of the blockhouse where George Catlin sat on a cannon breech painting portraits of Indian chiefs, thinking of

all the others who'd stood here before. Hugh Glass
hunted bighorn sheep on the bluffs across the Yellowstone. James Bridger spun some of his tales sitting in
the warm sun outside the gate. Sir George Gore burnt
his wagons here. Mike Fink shot Carpenter between
the eyes. All gone now, nothing left but ghosts and
memories, the river going on and on.

The last trapper working on contract for the American
Fur Company was Mountain Harry Yount.

In 1867 the army purchased what was left of Fort
Union, demolished it, and hired the steamer *Lulella*—
Grant Marsh at the helm—to carry the material down-
river to the confluence where they were building Fort
Buford, one of a chain of posts being built to keep the
hostiles in line.

When at last Tatanka-Iyotanka left Canada, he came
to Fort Buford and surrendered. He handed his rifle to
his son Crowfoot, who turned it over to Major D. H.
Brotherton of the Seventh Infantry, and said, "I wish it
to be remembered that I was the last man of my tribe to
surrender my rifle."

A few days later, stripped of his possessions and
dressed in ill-fitting white man's clothes, he was
marched aboard the steamer *General Sherman*, and
shipped down the river to the agency at Standing Rock.

Ten years later he was murdered by his own people,
the Indian Police, for his part in Wevoka's peyote
dream to ghost dance the earth clean of white men and
bring the buffalo back.

That winter the Seventh Cavalry revenged Custer's death by surrounding and slaughtering 146 Sioux men, women, and children—one gun among them—in the snow at Wounded Knee Creek. Twenty-three medals of honor were awarded.

Gerard said there was some music he wanted me to hear, and so while he cooked the venison I sat on a couch in the trailerhouse listening to Floyd Wetherman and Paul Ortega, Exile, and the Forty-Niners on the stereo. The albums had names like *Custer Died for Your Sins*, *Two Worlds*, and *Plight of the Redman*.

We build a fire for the sweat down in the riverbottom about a quarter mile from the fort and about ten yards from the water, clearing the snow away. Gerard cuts down ten young willows, each about as thick as my thumb, and forms a hoop out of two, binding them at either end with imitation sinew, which comes on a roll, just like string. He makes a dome with the rest of the willows and covers it with canvas. It's about three feet high and four feet across, just big enough for us to sit in. We put more wood on the fire and stand around talking, watching the rocks get hot. A pair of owls call to each other back and forth across the river. Mist rolls in over the gumbo bluffs.

"What do you want for your children?" I ask Gerard. He says he wants them to have a sense of their culture. He doesn't think they'll ever get the religion, there's just too much of a gap. Gerard's wife is German

Catholic. He won't force his religion on any of his family, he hopes they'll come to it themselves, on their own, though he doubts they will.

Gerard speaks what he calls broken Indian. Indians used to speak broken English, now they speak broken Indian. His grandfather and father could still speak Hidatsa, and so could he, a little bit. He spoke it well before he was sent from the reservation at Fort Berthold to a boarding school when he was eight. When he came back, he couldn't speak it at all and has been trying to relearn ever since, not just the language but all the old ways.

Last year he skinned a buffalo with a flint knife and built an earth lodge. It gave him respect for the old ladies, that's for sure. One of the reasons he is learning the old ways is that he believes he might need them to survive in the future. There was a prophet among his people who said he would return to the earth when the grass was turned upside-down, the Missouri was flowing north, and the antelope grew a fifth hoof—the first two of these have already taken place.

When the rocks in the fire are pulsing white, Gerard says it's time to go in. We strip, hanging our clothes on the brush. Gerard uses a shovel to take the rocks out of the fire and place them in the center of the lodge. When they're all inside, we enter, close the door, and sit cross-legged on deer hides.

The heat comes on gradually, and then intensely. All of the cold river days leave me in shudders.

Gerard asks how I'm doing and I say, "Fine, just fine,

just great," and then I say, "I'm going to pass out," and he throws open the door and we run outside.

The firelight blinds me and the cold air stuns. I stop, blinking, listening to Gerard splash into the river and come back up shouting. The moment my toes touch water, I dive.

We do it two more times, put our clothes on, and walk up through the willows and cottonwoods to a tipi near the fort. Gerard builds a fire, and his wife brings over a kettle of stew and a sack of fry-bread. I'm as relaxed, as weak and limber and at ease, as clean as I've ever been in my life. Neither of us feels like talking. After supper we roll up in buffalo robes on willow beds, lie looking out at the stars through the open vent flaps, watching the cottonwood smoke rise from the fire, and listening to the wind and blowing snow hit the tipi's sides, the flutter of ribbons tied up on the pole tops, and in the distance, infrequently, whenever the wind lulls or goes silent, the sound of a faraway pump jack, like a drum, beating.

YELLOWSTONE MAP: *Diane Essington*

TYPEFACE: *Granjon*

BOOK DESIGN: *Wilsted & Taylor*

JACKET DESIGN: *Wilsted & Taylor*

COMPOSITOR: *Wilsted & Taylor*

PRINTER: *Haddon Craftsmen*

BINDER: *Haddon Craftsmen*